Katie :) x

i

USA Trains Santa Fe F3, A & B units with Santa Fe Super Chief passenger stock in the garden of Sandy Lodge (Phil Johnson)

Images in this work are from a number of different sources, both private and manufacturers/suppliers – the use of manufacturer and supplier images is neither an endorsement of the manufacturer/supplier nor of the product illustrated. Further the author offers no recommendation of which type of equipment should or can be used in the design, production and operation of a garden railway.

Frontispiece: Roundhouse Vale of Rheidol "Owain Glyndwr" on David and Becky Pinniger's Ambledown Valley Railway.

.

Also by Roger J Mannion

The Duchess – Stanier's Masterpiece

The Streaks – Gresley's A4s

The Southern Pacific's - Bulleid's Radical Design

Published by Sutton Publishing

David Pinniger also wrote for

Garden Railway Magazine

And now writes for

16mm Today – The 16mm Association Society Magazine

A
Down To Earth
Railway

Building
Your Garden
Railway

Roger J Mannion

With Live Steam
Contributions
from
David Pinniger

Published by

Garden Railway Specialists Ltd

Copyright © Roger J Mannion & David Pinniger 2020

Roger J Mannion & David Pinniger have asserted their right to be identified as the authors of this work in accordance with Copyright, Designs and Patents Act 1988

First published 2020

A CIP Catalogue record for this book is available in the British Library

ISBN 978-1-913218-30-0

Printed and Bound by
Biddles Books Ltd

Contents

Preface

When I first considered a garden railway I thought how hard is this, I had already modelled in 00 gauge reasonable successfully, I was also putting an N gauge system together – so what is the difficulty, after all it is only a larger scale and there are likely issues with weather but all that can be dealt with, cannot be to many problems!

How many of us recognise this, starting off with bags of confidence, even a touch of arrogance, then reality starts to settle in, you put the first attempt at a plan on to paper, can I not tighten that curve, will my motive power transit that radius – so a bigger radius, but where? OK back to the drawing board, I think the track route is about right, what about electrics, the power source is where? I need to run a mains cable but wasn't I intending to put a tunnel there! And of course it goes on and on!

So finally truth becomes apparent, this is a long term project, and you do need to plan your railway properly, to understand not only what you wish your railway to look like but to make sure that it meets the mechanical, civil and electrical needs of your ideas, so that you have some chance of longevity and success. While we should accept that a railway is never really finished – you always feel the need to add some additional detail - you do also want to have the opportunity of watching the trains go by and of course having "bragging" rights with friends.

At the beginning of my build there were a limited number of areas offering advice, so it really was a matter of using the imperfect knowledge I had to move the design forward. I was lucky being a qualified electronic engineer, having a solid digital background also helped; nonetheless it was still a challenge. Yet it is not all bad news, the challenges are part of the pleasure in this hobby – no pain, no gain! Clearly a lot of mistakes were made, but then don't we all do the same and the lessons learnt provide a degree of satisfaction particularly when things go so horribly wrong but nonetheless you succeeded in the end.

This book is really the results of my experiences, my failures and mistakes, the help and advice I received which made me keep going despite my frustrations and screw ups. Hopefully the little I do know and the expertise of all I have spoken to will help others not to make the same mistakes – however I am sure we will still make new and/or other mistakes. Nevertheless I hope it will help, please let me know if there are any errors or additions and maybe a second edition could be produced in the future.

I would like to thank the following for their assistance, advice and help in producing this work. David Pinniger for his writings and assistance with the sections on Live Steam motive power – thank you David I have learnt a lot. Matthew and Michael Adamson of Garden Railway Specialists, without whose support this book would have unlikely to have been produced. A big thanks goes out to members of the garden railway fraternity for permission to use their copyright images and to the supporters of G Scale Central who allowed me to search their image libraries. All images are acknowledged where appropriate.

Finally I must thank my family for the support and understanding when I disappeared into the workshop or the railway, and for the hours being incommunicado during the writing stage. And finally, any errors in this work are solely my responsibility and cannot be put at the door of any of the contributors.

For those starting or planning to start, for those well into the design and those who are enjoying their labours watching the trains go by, I salute you and hope this work is of some interest and help.

Roger Mannion 2020.   blackfive23@googlemail.com

1. Introduction

What is a garden railway and is it always in the garden? Surprising questions for a book about this hobby of ours, or are they? The simple answer to both questions is that a garden railway is whatever you want it to be, it is your railway to run and enjoy. While garden railways consist predominantly of larger scale rolling stock, motive power and buildings, it does not have to be like that, garden railways can be in 0 scale or smaller, there are examples of railways in the garden running in 00 scale, however this is extremely unusual and a lot of the time less than practical. For this work we will consider the larger scales. Does the railway need to be outside, again the answer is no, it is what you wish it to be. I know of large scale railways which run completely undercover, this has the advantage of not having to deal with problems of the weather but to cater for this you do need a large building or shed to accommodate your railway! Nonetheless regardless of the design, gauge or scale it is a good idea to have part of your railway undercover, or at least some type of undercover storage/work area; a workshop, train/loco shed or motive power depot, this makes things easier to protect your stock and to carry out those running repairs, tests, modifications etc.

© 2020 Michael Adamson

The morning "stopper" calls at Gresford Station, hauled by
South Eastern and Chatham Railway (SECR) H Class 0-4-4T

So how did all of this Garden Railway malarkey start? In the early days during the turn of the 19th/20th century, model locomotives were produced by numerous different companies almost on a cottage industry level, consequently scale and gauge compatibility was not really considered, making it extremely difficult to share the hobby or to run different manufacturers models on your new railway. This was not to change until the late 19th century when the Märklin Company of Nüremberg proposed a set of standard gauges & scales with very imaginative & original titles; gauge 1, 2, & 3! Gauge 1 being the smallest and gauge 3 the largest. Nonetheless this was a major step forward for our hobby with the new scales/gauges adopted by most of the European and some of the US manufacturers. However with the end of the 1st world war, the depression and a general change in how the world was seen, the railways in gauge 1 and larger became much less popular, primarily because of space and cost grounds. During this period companies like The Lionel Company and the American Flyer in the US, plus Hornby and Bassett Lowke in the UK produced a new gauge, gauge 00, what is today known as H0 in the Europe/US, it took off due to the relatively low cost and the ability to run these trains indoors.

As the new century progressed the hobby started to abandon railways in the garden, with the exception of a few who had larger gardens and the wherewithal to finance the larger scales in the open. However the majority of the enthusiasts' modelled railways indoors, using the smaller scales. This situation really wasn't to change significantly until the 1960's when the German toy company, Ernst Paul Lehmann commenced marketing plastic locomotives and rolling stock to the scale of 1:22.5 running on gauge 1 track. The stock was designed specifically for outdoor use having protected motors and gears etc., built utilizing rugged plastic construction. Initially German narrow gauge models were produced but the range eventually was to encompass US and other European motive power. These models were to become known as LGB (Lehmann Grossbahn). We now have gained a little understanding about how garden railways evolved; all we have to do is get started on our garden railway!

The commencement for any garden railway is you have ideas, plans, and aspirations for a layout of which the size is too big for your railway room, workshop, garage, loft. You may wish for greater realism, prototypical running or just relish something larger! So the obvious answer is to move to the garden. Of course, it is also possible that you do not like to model the smaller gauges and have always yearned for the big outdoors. Now of course with that decision made you really need to visit the whole question of garden railway, scale, gauge and outline, more of which later. At this point of course the most important decision is to have the families' agreement!

2. The Beginning

So we have this great idea for a garden railway, maybe a family present of some rolling stock or a locomotive, perhaps a long considered notion and now you are starting to have the time to really get to grips with the idea, so where do we start?

This is probably one of the most important stages and enjoyable, however get it wrong here, it will come back and "bite" you when you least expected it, typically when the track is down with the electrics plus the control systems in place! Think carefully at this point about what you really want with your railway, and it is your railway, so it can be whatever you wish it to be. This is the fun part, putting your ideas down, planning your special layout, working out the dream. Take your time and try to get it right now; it is much easier to correct paper or software layouts than the real thing, especially when the track bed etc. has been dug and laid in the garden. A very obvious statement I can hear you say, however you would be surprised at the number of people who get carried away by their enthusiasm. Clearly there will be opportunities to add to the layout at a later date, we all recognise that our railway is never really finished. However major modifications after the majority of the work has been completed will create extensive difficulties and are best designed out at the very beginning. Plan three times over but build once! Remember to consider your budget and try, it is hard I appreciate, to keep within budget. If your

© 2020 Michael Adamson

A Busy Scene as No.7812 "Erlestoke Manor" approaches Mickleton Station with a mixed goods

aspirations exceed your budget then design with the ability to expand in the future as your finances allow. One of your first considerations, before you put anything down on paper, certainly before you start the build, is to understand who/what this railway is for; you, the family, your children/grandchildren or will it be a layout which can be put out as an example "of how to" on social media? These will impact what the railway will look like, how it is run and consequently how it all goes together.

Marshal your thoughts and ideas, sketch out some rough layout concepts, try and get a handle on what you want, which scale, which gauge, the type of layout etc. What sort of railway do you really want, prototypical or freelance; narrow gauge, branch line, mainline or a mixture of all three? There is the additional issue of outline, do you wish your railway to be US, European, British or freelance. The site and route for your railway should also be assessed at this stage, do you want the track at a high level for ease of use or at ground level, remember the knees and joints, as age creeps on! Gradients also need to be considered for the motive power you are running.

If this in itself is not enough it is essential to review how the railway is to be powered, dc, battery, live steam; and controlled; analogue dc, digital or radio control; all of these will impact the design and are best inputted at this stage. Overlaying all of this is the question, as noted earlier, "who is the railway for?" Further you will need to think of the maintainability of your railway, in particular access; all of these will impact your design.

LGB Spreewald Locomotive

At the design stage you will have some ideas on the type of railway you want and this will help decide on the outline and the gauge of the railway. So what do gauge and outline mean, what is the difference between gauge and scale?

The outline is fairly straight forward, it is the shape, the style of the motive power and rolling stock; locomotives, coaches & goods stock. British outline is as it says typical of the UK railway system, including steam, diesel and electric power with the associated rolling stock. USA outline again includes diesel, steam and electric power with associated stock. Both the USA and British outlines include narrow gauge railways, typically Ffestiniog and the Lynton & Barnstable, plus in the USA, mining and logging lines. The European outline is predominately German, but also includes other countries, such as France, Switzerland

LGB DR Coach

and Austria as well as embracing narrow gauge & rack railways. Once a decision is made on outline it is probably best to be consistent across your complete railway. Although having a "neutral" outline railway does mean that you can run whatever you wish! Within the outline you may also wish to consider the time period of your layout, as this is your railway you could consider no specific time period, this does at least give you the opportunity to run any number of different types of motive power and rolling stock. Couple this with a "neutral" outline and you would have complete flexibility; nonetheless this is your railway so it is completely your decision.

Clearly the outline that you run will help decide on the gauge of your railway, prototypically most British, USA and European railways run on standard gauge track (4ft 8½in) nonetheless there are a number of differing narrow gauge railways running on anything from 2ft - 3ft 6ins, in addition however some European lines also have "meter" gauge! And then of course to add to the muddle the Irish Railways run on a 5ft 3in gauge known as broad gauge although nothing as wide as Brunel's 7ft ¼in broad gauge. All in all this can be a complex puzzle for the modeller.

USA Trains Canadian National SD70 MAC

So in terms of garden railways what is gauge? Gauge is the distance between the inside of the rails and is normally measured in millimetres (mm), hence 32mm, 45mm and 64mm. By and large the rail gauge reflects the scale of the motive power and rolling stock; I say this with some trepidation as a number of manufacturers' use the same gauge track for different and dissimilar scales. Typical of this is the USA Trains, Big Boy and Hudson locomotives, which are to 1:29 scale, running on 45 mm track. While this is claimed to be Gauge1 it is marginally different yet still running on the same track scale as that which is commonly understood to be Gauge 1, nominally 1:32. Likewise it is also true that not only do some manufacturers produce narrow gauge (NG) stock using 32mm track but also run NG stock on 45mm track! You can understand how new enthusiasts to the hobby can get confused! Many of these differences are the result of history when in early days, differing manufacturers built to the scale they found it easier to build to, without necessarily making any concessions to other companies.

USA Trains Union Pacific Caboose

In terms of scale, this is the representative size compared to the prototypical locomotive, truck, coach etc. being modelled. In garden railway terms these are typically 1:22.5, 1:29 & 1:32; thus 1:22.5 is 22.5 times smaller than the prototype, while 1:29 is 29 times smaller than the prototype and similarly with 1:32 being 32 times smaller. Thus it can be seen that locomotives of these scales, while running on the same 45mm gauge track, would have significant differences in actual model size, hence the need to be aware of these differences. Just to further muddy the waters, LGB, one of the more well-known European manufacturers, produces models in 1:22.5 scale which is claimed to provide the equivalent of prototypical meter gauge (1000mm track gauge), these models also run on 45mm track. Consequently, the rolling stock and motive power will have size differences, if compared with NG or standard gauge stock running on 45 mm track. At the end of the day you run your railway how you wish it to be, so scale, gauge & outline are completely yours to choose and if you wish to mix them, then it is your railway!

Track can and is also measured by the rail height in hundredths of an inch and known as code xxx, consequently code 250 is 0.250inch and code 332 is 0.332inch; a list of typical rail manufacturers with gauge and code is shown below. The greater rail height, i.e. code 332, is probably better for garden railways, as it tends to be more stable and easier to lay. However if you plan to have narrow gauge then you are likely to use 32mm track which can be appreciably different in height; typically code 200, this will be examined in more detail further within this work.

N Scale	HO Scale	On30 Scale	O Scale	Large Scale
1:160	1:87	1:48	1:48	1:22.5 or 1:20.3

Bachmann Train Scales
(On30 track is a scale 3 feet wide with 0 gauge scale stock)

© 2018 Roger Mannion

A Question of Scale.
The Author's USA Trains SD70 Mac, 1:29 scale, running on 45 mm track with Geoff Heald's Welsh Highland Line narrow gauge Princess 1:19 scale running on 32 mm track

1:32 SCALE
OFTEN REFERRED TO AS GAUGE 1
PROTOTYPE:
STANDARD GAUGE MAINLINE
4' 8 1/2" GAUGE

1:22.5 SCALE
KNOWN AS 'LGB' OR 'G' SCALE
PROTOTYPE:
EUROPEAN NARROW GAUGE
TYPICALLY METRE GAUGE

1:20.3 SCALE
15mm = 1 FOOT SCALE
PROTOTYPE:
3 FOOT NARROW GAUGE
TYPICAL USA NARROW GAUGE

|←—45mm—→|
RUNS ON 45mm GAUGE TRACK

|←—45mm—→|
RUNS ON 45mm GAUGE TRACK

|←—45mm—→|
RUNS ON 45mm GAUGE TRACK

Popular Scales and Gauges fig 1

1:19 SCALE
16mm = 1 FOOT SCALE
PROTOTYPE:
ENGLISH NARROW GAUGE
TYPICALLY 2' 6" - 3' GAUGE

1:13.7 SCALE
7/8 OF AN INCH = 1FT
PROTOTYPE:
2 FOOT NARROW GAUGE
TYPICALLY INDUSTRIAL RAILWAYS

1:19 SCALE
16mm = 1 FOOT SCALE
PROTOTYPE:
ENGLISH NARROW GAUGE
FOR 2 FOOT GAUGE

|←—45mm—→|
RUNS ON 45mm GAUGE TRACK

|←—45mm—→|
RUNS ON 45mm GAUGE TRACK

|←—32mm—→|
RUNS ON 32mm GAUGE TRACK

Popular Scales and Gauges fig 2

To make it simpler, in this work, we will consider G scale, both 45 mm & 32mm, plus Gauge 1, which in the UK is considered to be prototypically Standard Gauge (4ft 8½in). These sizes cover most of scales used in Garden Railways and despite disparity in the scales of the stock being used does provide some size relationship. Of course these differences can lead to problems with buildings, signals, loco crew & passengers having different sizes because of scale, when mixed on the same railway, so be aware! A comparison of track gauge, material and codes is shown below; for further details on gauge – v – scale, see appendix 6.

Aristo-Craft	45mm Brass Track	code 332 rail
	45mm Stainless Steel Track	code 332 rail (not so readily available)
Accucraft	45mm Brass Track	code 332 rail
	45mm Brass Track	code 250 rail
LGB	45mm Brass Track	code 332 rail
Piko	45mm Brass Track	code 332 rail
Peco	32mm Nickel Silver Track	code 200 rail (SM32)
	45mm Nickel Silver Track	code 200 rail (G1)
	45mm Nickel Silver Track	code 250 rail (G45)

Track Manufacturers Gauge, Material & Code Comparison

Having understood the scale/gauge conundrum we now need to think about what type of railway we would like. In its simplest form the layout will either be an out and back or a circuit. Within these it is possible to have a number of differing styles of railway, including but not limited to, a shunting/goods railway, a branch line, a mainline or all three; the layout can run on standard gauge; or narrow gauge of any of the differing track sizes within those gauges. Having made an initial decision on the track, consideration should then be given to the outline, period, traction type wanted; this will also feed back into the scale and gauge debate.

Having now spent time researching and determining the preliminary plan it is time to get outside and look at where your railway is going to go, in the garden. At this point it is doubly important that you talk to your family about what is going to happen, if your family has plans for that corner of the garden that you are planning to dig up for track bed, it does not bode well for the future of a successful railway – or partnership!

This is the time to think about how you intend to install the track; at ground level or at a height. Building at a height has some advantages, aging joints do not complain as much when the layout is off the ground, the railway always look better at eye level, and by lifting it above the garden it does not interfere so much with the planting and the maintenance of the garden. Nonetheless serious consideration also needs to be given to any possible gradients which may be required. While a 1:20 gradient is possible, it is not really advisable and gradients of 1:50 should be considered the maximum.

The track gradient can also be expressed as a percentage; this is calculated by measuring the maximum height of the gradient and dividing that by the length over which the gradient raises to the maximum. This number is multiplied by 100 to provide the percentage.

H/L x 100 = % gradient

H = maximum height of gradient
L = length of gradient to maximum height

It is possible to run your railway with a gradient of 4% but is not advisable – 2% should be considered the maximum. Nevertheless the amount of gradient will also depend upon the railway that you are operating. A mainline railway designed to have a 4% gradient would be out of place, even the Lickey Bank which is the steepest adhesion mainline in the UK is only 2.65%. However if you are running a logging line, gradients, prototypically would be steep, maybe up to 4.5%, likewise rack railways are up to 48% - note LGB rack locomotives are designed for 25% gradients, but more on rack railways later.

With all gradient design you must make sure that the initial approach to the gradient is not sharp but a gentle transition which gradually increases the slope, further it is important that the whole of the gradient is smooth without dips or bumps, this applies both on a raising and a falling gradient. Clearly a smooth transition from flat to up gradient is important but this also applies to the transition from the up gradient to flat and up/flat to the down gradient – all changes must be smooth and as gradual as possible. Also note that during gradient transitions couplings can become detached depending upon the coupling used and the gradient. LGB 64462 coupler hooks are used with rack railways to overcome any risk of this happening and can be used on regular "flat" sections of your railway.

A further point to be aware of with gradients is the use of curved gradients as there is already a limitation on the speeds for certain size locomotives on curved sections of track plus there is the addition of increased friction etc. So if possible curved gradients should be avoided but in any case should be limited, typical radius limitations are shown below. These are shown as track radius codes against a percentage of gradients and are the recommended maximum radius for the given gradient, percentage shown.

Radius 1 = 2% Gradient
Radius 2 = 2.25% Gradient
Radius 3 = 2.50% Gradient

Rack railways are of course a special case and will be discussed later within this work.

Before leaving the subject of gradients, one further note; be aware that live steam locomotives should avoid gradients unless they have a good radio control, as steaming up & down gradients needs significant adjustment of regulator and gear to avoid damage or stalling, not to mention the issues with firebox water levels.

Having looked at some of the issues in planning your railway it would be wise now to produce a scale plan of the garden, with measurements, so that subsequently you can superimpose your railway ideas onto that plan. Always make sure that the scale of your drawing matches that of any system, (software/paper) you are using to produce the final design. Consideration should also be given to taking some images of the various parts of the garden that you wish to "drive" your railway though. While thinking about the plans in the garden deliberation should also be given to providing a motive power depot, shed or workshop, in which to store the locos and rolling stock, as well as carrying out maintenance and repairs. Finally before disappearing inside to start the design ask yourself is your railway practical, think maintenance, now and in the future; will your chosen motive power run properly; is there enough space and will it work?

So you have decided on the scale, the time period, outline and gauge/type of track; you have completed the back of a "fag packet" design, compared that with the real garden area and found that it seems to work; so now is the time for the design proper.

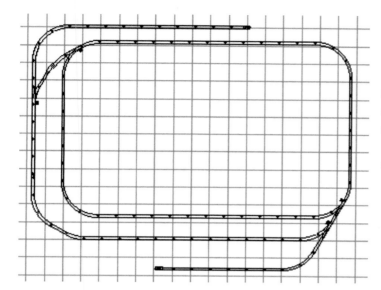

This squared layout with open centre is excellent for running around a flowerbed, fish pond, or other centrepiece.

Requires approximately 18' by 16'.

Before the design is started some thoughts need to be given about how the plan is to be prepared; a simple paper design using conventional drawing instruments or the use of computer based design packages. There are any numbers of software packages out there, some highly detailed and expensive CAD packages, while others can be as complex or as basic as you wish. Make absolutely sure that any package you plan to use has the correct track libraries and if possible have objects – trees, buildings, signals etc., of the correct scale and outline for your railway. Not all of these packages have G scale 45mm/32mm or SM32 track. A lot of the packages are designed for the smaller scales. Two typical packages that are available are *AnyRail* and *SCARM*; both have the advantage that they are free to download. Clearly readers use these at their own risk.

How the railway is laid out including the component parts need to be properly thought through at this time and this will directly relate to the railway you are running, the scale and type of track. The position of points, sidings, stations etc., will need to be understood and sited correctly. We have briefly referred to gradients and while in general 1:50 should not cause major constraints it will very much be conditional on the motive power used and the load behind the draw bar. Prototypically gradients were an issue for steam and diesel motive power, requiring bankers, dependent upon loadings, Lickey and Shap come to mind in this country, consequently unless you wish to have the operational interest of adding bankers to your service train, thought is needed.

Curves are another consideration which must be worked out prior to starting to build, while a lot of locomotive manufacturers give the minimum radius curve as approximately 2ft, not all motive power is going to be able to negotiate these sharp curves. In fact it is very likely, despite alternative claims, that a 2ft minimum curve will create significant difficulties to both motive power and rolling stock. Certainly the larger steam locomotives would have difficulties, particularly those without a leading pony truck or bogie. Even the power bogies of diesel or electric stock would suffer problems. Consideration should therefore be given to using 4ft or greater radius curves where possible. As a general rule use the greatest radii possible consistent with the size and space for your layout. Clearly with narrow gauge layouts and the reduced size of motive power associated with these types of layouts, the minimum radii can be adjusted to suit the requirements of the smaller design. In all cases, depending upon your motive power, wagons, coaches etc., it is highly recommended that you add transition curves on entering tight radii, these slow the change from straight to curved track, providing a smooth linear motion, going into and out of the curve. These transitions will also help to avoid locking rolling stock on curves; in particular when you have corridor stock, close coupled rolling stock or goods wagons buffered up.

These can be tricky to implement and on the prototype railway requires significant computing power to calculate the continuously varying radius at both the entry and exit of high speed curves, on our railway we do not need to go to that degree of detail. However the use of transition curves will ease any problems of lurching or bad running at curves particularly where, because of a lack of space, the ideal radius is not possible.

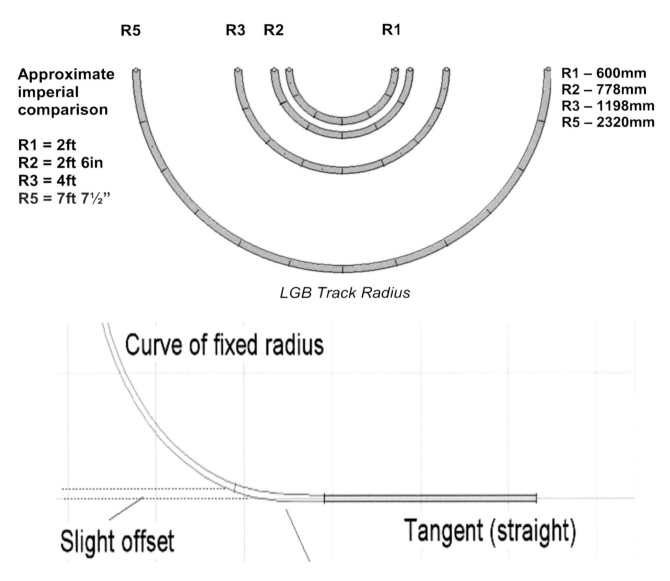

LGB Track Radius

Transition or Easement Curve

Rather than going from a straight section directly to a curve use a short length of flexible track to where you wish the curve to start, the geometry can be tedious so using your eye to determine the transition will work, (note that the human, mark one eyeball, is very good at seeing inconsistencies!). To assist in this, use a length of some type of flexible plastic to mark the lie of the track on the ground, plastic flat curtain runner is good for this. Secure it at the end of your straight and then bend to meet with the start of the curve, subsequently when the transition looks good pin to the track bed until you have marked out the route.

A further refinement for your railway curves is the application of super-elevation; this is prototypical and raises the outer rail of the curve over the inner rail. The amount of super elevation increases from zero at the start of the curve to its highest point at the apex and subsequently decreases back to zero at the end of the curve. For garden railways the increase in height for super-elevation is measured in millimetres and will only have significant impact if you are running high speed stock on curves. Consequently the work involved in achieving this may not be considered worthy of the return. Nonetheless it does give a very pleasing effect. On the prototypical railway it is used to reduce wheel and flange wear plus improve passenger comfort.

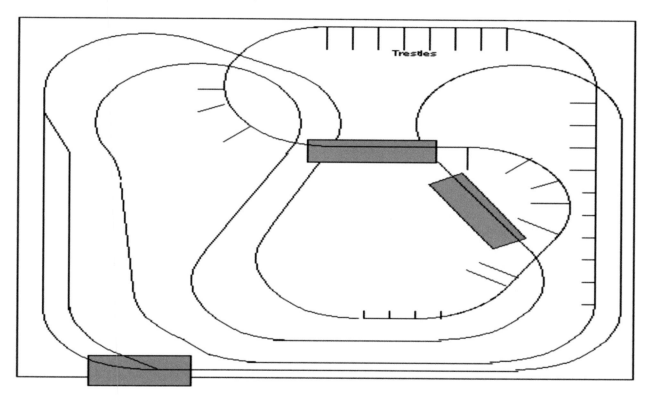

Initial Simple Track Plan

Normally your design will be able to be constructed using set track but if flexible track lengths are used, take care to make sure that the recommended radii are not exceeded. With all track work it is important to get it right now rather than have to lift track which has previously been laid because it is found that motive power cannot traverse it. By the same definition, point work needs to be laid correctly so as to match the correct radii of the interconnecting track work. For sake of consistency the details for track work shown refer to 45mm code 332 track however the principles will be common for other track sizes. When using LGB 45mm track there are a number of additional planning measurements which need to be taken into consideration – LGB 45mm track is used here as it tends to be representative and is common in Europe and the UK, other makes of 45mm track will have similar dimensional considerations. Lineside constructions, platforms, signal boxes etc. need to have a minimum of 2.5inches clearance from the track centres, tunnel/bridge heights should be a minimum of 8.5inches, this maybe higher dependent upon the motive power and rolling stock that is operated. If a tunnel is to be part of the layout make sure that it is only two arm lengths long or if longer, has a lift off section providing access to the track; if anything is going to derail or fail, it will do so in the tunnel (Murphy's Law)! The minimum spacing between adjacent tracks should be 6.5inches from the track centres – this must be more on curves to allow for motive power and rolling stock overhang as the train negotiates the bend. This will of course include trains in both directions, particularly on curves.

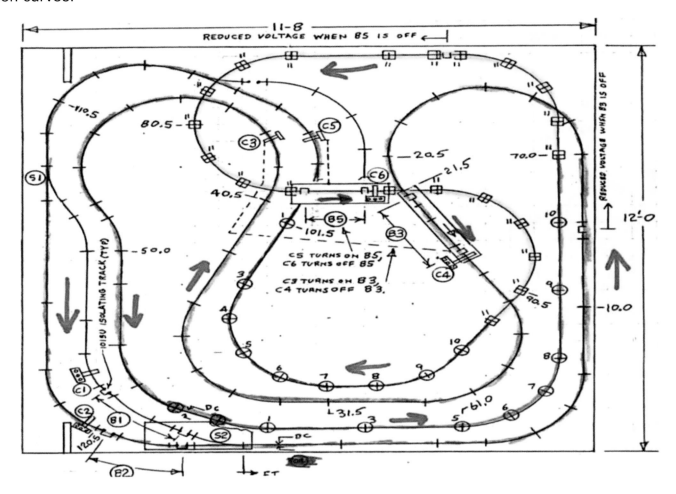

Simple track plan detailed

Your plan must also identify if your railway is to have control and what that control will be. Initially this may just take the form of a simple dc supply with control from a simple analogue power unit which is connected directly to the track. This method of using the rails to provide power for your railway is a really straight forward way to initially test that your plan does really does do what it says it should and that no hidden gremlins are apparent. Regardless of which final method of control you decide upon, carrying out an initial "simple" test run prior to finalising you power system can save significant heartache later in the build process, however more of this later.

Nonetheless your plan should show how the railway is to be powered and controlled, if powered electrically then the source of the power should also be shown, house, garage, workshop etc. Likewise information should be given on how points, signals will work; are these to be manually changed, e.g. using wire in tube, rods; or with motors, if motors which type and make? Do not forget differing makes of motors have different sizes and means of connection to the device to be controlled; this will need to be accommodated. Additionally will the motors be changed with switches or programmed via DCC; if the latter

16

consideration of what type of decoder is used and where these will be sited is needed. The plan will also want to identify any other control modules typically signal control, automatic braking, automatic reversing and reverse loop etc. Clearly if your railway motive power is battery powered or live steam then this also has to be acknowledged on the plan. The use of live steam will likely need the provision of a "steam up" bay, consideration within the plan will should to be given to this.

Before you complete the design stage you also need to review what your railway is to look like, do you want tunnels, or bridges; are you going to include a water feature? What infrastructure features do you want; a station, goods yard, branch line, loco shed etc.? The impact of all and any infrastructure features must be understood and catered for at this point so that you can be assured the track and space to provide for these features is available. Clearly some compromises will be needed but modifications are simple at this point of the design. You do not want to be attempting an extensive rebuild or redesign when the railway is running and all completed!

Finally you need to review the types of electronic modules you are using, (if any) and their protection against the environment - rain & snow etc. Are they fully water proof or do they need protection, disguised with buildings or covered in some way? This information will impact the space you have available and what you do with the scenics of the railway.

The design stage is now all but completed; however you also need to think about some outdoors considerations. The first is the environment in the garden, are there trees which are going to drop leaves, debris etc. onto the track? Are there any damp parts of the garden which your railway is going to pass though, and what is the impact? Is drainage likely to be an issue? Then the maintenance issues, can the garden still be supported, remember you are sharing the garden with your family so the seasonal maintenance of this must be considered as part of your plan. Equally as important, can the track, railway structures etc., be maintained without major disturbance to the existing garden? If the answer to all of the conditions and requirements outlined above are yes then you are ready to move outside and begin the construction of your railway. Despite all of this initial planning there will invariable be some problems but by putting this amount of effort in at the very beginning you should be able to overcome most of the major difficulties, the problems you are likely to face will then hopefully, be relatively small.

3. The Build

David Pinniger's Snowdon Bwlch

We have now got to the stage of the hard work and the build but first thoughts needs to be given as to who will be doing the work, in particular the initial hard, ground work; for instance if you are going to run your railway at ground level and you are intent upon ballasting the track prototypically with ballast and a trench, possibly having a local contractor in, with a machine to dig the trench, could be an option, or it is possible these days to hire a self-drive, small machine for a day or more, this is a further option. Clearly these options will very much depend upon budget and the size of both your railway and your garden. Inviting a friend or member of the family to help is maybe a cheaper alternative and would also likely encourage longer term participation. With railways that are constructed above the ground, this issue is not so much of a problem. This is the type of decision that needs to be taken into account now, before the heavy work starts.

Before you get down to the hard work in the garden it is important to appreciate that track laying should be undertaken with great care. Check levels with a spirit level, both across the rails and forwards and backwards; make sure gradients are suitable for your motive power and that the curves are as long as possible, consistent with space and rolling stock. Taking time and care with laying the track at this stage will pay dividends when the railway is complete. Whether the railway is to be above ground or to lie on the ground, the first stage must be to mark out the route using stakes or similar, at suitable intervals, it is useful to have previously cut, full size card templates of points and curves. These will make sure that the course of the railway on the ground not only matches your plan but will also provide satisfactory running for the rolling stock without awkward joints or track angles. I have found that marking out this way with the addition of a white powder line interconnecting each stake and the card point/curve templates really helps to visualise the track layout and enables the correction of issues before the ground work commences. I have used cheap cooking flour; this is environmentally friendly and also will be easily dispersed when the track bed is completed, thus not upsetting the gardener in the family!

18

Checking the Gradients and Levels

Using building blocks for the gradients

When finally transferring the plan makes sure that the trains do not disappear behind plants trees etc., at least not for too long, you want to enjoy the success of all your work with the train being seen. At this point with the layout shown on the ground, stand back, review the route you are proposing, check that it does match you aspirations, change things if you feel it is not right. It is easy to move a stake, modify a flour route or change the position of a point or curve template then redesign the track bed having once dug it! You will likely find the task ahead daunting but do not rush, enjoy, take one step at a time, thus by checking & double checking you will end up with the railway you desire.

Your track must be laid on a good foundation which will provide little movement, deal with the environment and also the need to maintain the garden, whether it is weeding, lawn mowing or just access with garden tools. Drainage and protection from vegetation or local pets and wild life must be incorporated at this stage. Remember your track has to survive all that the weather can throw at it and still successfully run your train service.

4. Ground Level

The prototype railway has been laying track for 100's of years and it maybe that you would wish to follow their method; however with garden railways there is never a one size fits all solution. Most of the railways have a mixture of track bed methods to meet the differing conditions found in the garden. If you put 15 garden railway enthusiasts in a room and ask for a ballasting solution you will get 15 different answers! With the power of the web solutions to the problems can now be readily sourced on line. The illustration discussed below is but one example of many; a combination of all or even none is perfectly acceptable, after all it is your railway!

© 2018 Jim Berry

Cutting the soil for the Track Bed

Floating Ballast

This is a very similar method to prototype railways but may not be suitable for all of your permanent way. A trench approximately 4 inches deep needs to be dug with a width of roughly twice the track width, this is the width across the sleepers not the rail. A good dose of propriety weed killer should be applied throughout the trench but take care not to harm associated garden plants or tree roots etc. Plus make sure that children and pets are kept well away. The trench should be lined with a good, long life weed suppression membrane – ideally one with at least 5 years of life. The life can be increased by laying old newspaper under the membrane, 4/5 sheets thick will suffice. Make sure that drainage holes are made though the membrane at suitable distances so that the trench does not end up flooded.

At this stage you need to consider providing for cabling which will be used to power your railway and the auxiliaries such as signals, point motors, lights etc., you may also wish to consider how power is to be feed to the track, perhaps you want to install some form of power bus from which "droppers" can be added to connect to the track. This does increase reliability of power supply; particularly with the impact the weather can have on the track. Nonetheless, however you plan to connect services, control and/or power, now is the time to provide a small channel or flexible conduit into which the cables can be laid, we will discuss size and types of cables later but at this point it is better to have oversized and allow for too many cables then too few, so always overestimate the requirements. Digging up the trench to lay extra cable, with the track in place is not advisable.

© 2018 Jim Berry

Ballast & some track laid – initial test of the electrics

With the use of live steam motive power, you may consider that the need for cable laying is redundant, this may be true however remember that lighting, both for buildings and stations etc. could be a useful addition, plus of course operating signals and points with power control is worth thinking about at this stage.

Before infilling the trench with your ballast some form of edging should be put in place so that grass can be mown and the garden maintained, additionally it will reduce the problems of weeds and over hanging vegetation interfering with the track. The edging should be the best you can afford, ideally constructed of metal to give longevity, this should be placed so that the top of the edging is at the "cut" grass height or the maximum height of the surrounding soil, this will allow mowers to be able to cut the lawn without damaging the edging and will stop soil falling onto the track.

© 2018 Meika Ltd

Easy Lawn Edging in Brown
by Smartedge on Primrose.co.uk website.

The trench can then be infilled with about 3 - 3½ inches deep of sharp rough chippings these can be crushed rock, shingle or chippings, in fact any rough ballast will be OK. The point is that it has to knit together and provide a firm base. If budget or the supply of gravel is an issue, old bricks or breeze blocks can be used to fill the lower part of the trench, then infill over the top with your chippings. The use of pea gravel or other rounded stones is not advised as it will not lock together but rather roll about and cause the track to move under load. With the track bed base filled it will need to be tramped down firmly so that there are no undulations or voids which will cause the track to sag. Jiggling a large screwdriver or similar tool in the ballast will help to get the stones to fill voids and dips while a piece of wood, to the width of the trench, struck with a club hammer, along the length of the trench will firm up the base track bed. Tedious this maybe but doing this with care will provide a good long lasting foundation for the permanent way.

Having completed the base track bed you can now lay the ballast for the track, this needs to be a liberal amount so that the track can be agitated and held by the ballast. Think about the colour and size of this material. Size is important but using scale ballast may not be successful, it needs to match your motive power but be of a sufficient size to lock the track in place. Colour is also something which needs to be considered, bright garish ballast will look out of place and spoil any effect you are trying to create. Do not forget that over the years ballast will weather, with colours mellowing. Typically the use of potting grit from good garden centres has been used with success; this tends to be from 2 - 5mm diameter.

A simpler but less pleasing method is to use bricks or concrete blocks set into the trench to just below the top, again these need to be secure and laid very firmly, creating a solid foundation for your track. The track is then loosely secured to the blocks/bricks using brass screws, followed with a top up of ballast which can then be tramped to allow around and under the track, a degree of float.

© 2018 Jim Berry

Ballasting the Trench

There are a number of differing methods of applying the track ballast one method is to dry mixed with cement and sand, say at ratio of 3:1:1, grit, sand and cement. Subsequently applied to the track, and then gently sprayed with water. Gently is important else you risk washing the sand and cement away. Whether it is laid dry or with cement, the ballast must first be jiggled around, between and under the track so that the track is gripped firmly, work in with a brush and make sure that no mounds or dips exist, agitating the track will help to achieve this. Having completed the ballast make sure that it is not going to interfere with the running of the rolling stock or the operations of points etc. Only then apply water if it is intended to be used. This can be a painstaking method which is hard on the knees but if carried out correctly will provide a realistic effect. Dependent upon where you live you may need to allow for the track itself to have the capability to expand and contract as a result of temperature changes because of the weather. Take this into consideration during the track laying. Finally make absolutely sure that any ballast does not foul your locos or points etc. and that it is secure enough not to be disturbed when carrying out routine garden maintenance. In some respects this procedure will be a "check it and see operation" but however the track bed is worked, it is essential that the track is secured and meets the requirements of your railway.

Wooden Track bed

At ground level you can also lay track using pressure treated wood such as decking pieces, modern pressure treated wood is normally guaranteed for at least 10 years so should last if treated regularly and maintained. These wood sections can be laid over paved areas etc., where a solid base for the wood can be provided; this is useful when crossing existing hard based areas of your garden. These wood track layers can also be used to compensate for any varying heights of terrain in your garden; it is a fairly simple task to lay the wooden sections over dips or undulations using treated posts as supports. The use of screws into the wood section will of course open the wood to the elements however pressure treat material has a greater resistance to this danger and using brass screws will help reduce the corrosive effects.

©2018 Shelia Trentini

Wooden base for a curved track bed

Of course it is also possible to lay your track directly to the decking in the garden, it is debatable if this is completely successful, not because of the fixing and mechanics but more because your deck would have been constructed for the quiet evening drink or meal with the family, not for the railway to be running all over it, nonetheless – it is your railway……. only be aware that your family may not agree!

© 2018 Slawman

The Deck Line

A layer of roofing felt of appropriate colour and texture can be used to cover the wooden track base. This will provide two important advantages, the first to increase the protection of your wooden base, because despite how well it is originally treated it will be affected by the weather, covering helps to decrease this risk; secondly if added aesthetically it will help to match the track bed with the ballast. If you really wanted the track bed to match that which had previously been laid you could fix a thin strip of flexible material to the sides of the wooden base, extend this a few mm higher than the base to form a shallow channel to lay the ballast applied previously. This is your railway so you can make it as you want to. By using a wooden base it does make the layout just a little easier to route and set up, particularly with control cables etc. which can be attached to the underside of the wooden base. However wooden track bed for curves needs to be thought though and a different approach used. See more on this when we discuss raised layouts.

Typical raised track base using concrete slaps and posts cemented into the ground

Concrete Base

You may also wish to consider laying track on a concrete base which is suitably ballasted, a trench will have to be dug for this, of similar dimensions to that for the floating ballast foundations, while this is as labour intensive as for using floating ballast it does give, if correctly completed, a greater longevity to the track bed onto which track can be secured firmly, followed by a light layer of ballast set on top of the concrete for aesthetic reasons. However be aware of issues regarding drainage because you could be building yourself a gully for the rain water to flow through – not ideal! Further you will also need to give due consideration to how control and power cables are laid because once the concrete is in and if you bury cable within the concrete, it will be an extremely tedious job to get to these, add more or be forced to replace them because of pests. As with the floating ballast, it is advisable that side edging should be included to reduce the creep of weeds, vegetation etc. and to allow mowing of lawns. Also note should be made of the risk of track movement due to temperature changes, whether hot or cold, consequently securing track to a concrete base needs to be carried out with this in mind. One further issue with concrete track beds is that once it is down, it is down; change your mind subsequently regarding the layout and route, at your peril!

A slightly less onerous method is to use concrete blocks laid on a firm concrete foundation and set firmly with mortar. Track can be secured directly to the blocks and a covering of ballast applied – try to avoid the use of Thermalite, or similar blocks as these absorb moisture and will fail because of it.

A scene from Dave Lawrence's G Scale Society garden open day, on track laid on a stone base.

Of course it is also possible to lift the track off the ground to cope with undulations using brick, stone or concrete block construction. Depending upon the type of material used, the raised bed could be infilled with earth, planted or grassed over to form an attractive embankment which would be prototypical. However if the railway is to be laid on this type of base for the whole route then you have to be very clear about the where the layout goes and how it will fit together, making changes later will incur significant penalties in terms of frustration and hard work.

In reality our railways are normally built to our grand scheme and designed to fit within the contours of garden itself. Thus it is highly likely that if your railway is planned to be at or near ground level then all of the above methods will be used to build the track bed in one part or other, if for no other reason than to deal with the differing levels within the garden but more likely to add scenic appeal.

Concrete based track on Dave Lawrence's Railway

*Multi-track layout showing the goods shed at the terminus station
on Stuart Cakebread's live steam railway*

5. Raised Track

Clearly having a track which sits 2ft – 3ft above ground level has a number of advantages, not least that you can sit down and watch your trains go by! The track can be built clear of any plants, weeds and pets' etc. while the maintenance of the garden will be able to be continued with limited interference to the railway. The construction itself is simplified and the addition of control or power cables is relatively straightforward. However this construction design does limit the ability to provide scenery, buildings sidings etc. without a significant amount of additional wood work and support. Nonetheless I personally prefer this type of construction, possibly because if I do get it wrong it is fairly straightforward to change, or maybe I can work wood or plastic a lot better than working stone or concrete. Of course it helps being that much higher of the ground – it helps to save the knees and the back!

© 2018 Eoin Callinan

Wooden post, treated and cemented into ground

Typically the track bed for a single line should be laid on approximately 6 inches wide flat timber boards which have been pressure treated to resist the effects of the weather. These are then attached to approximately 75mm square or larger, treated wooden posts secured into the ground. These can either be secured by appropriately sized holes and cement or by the use of the heavy gauge metal spikes driven into the ground and which secure the posts with bolts, typically Metposts or similar. The vertical posts need to be installed at 24inch – 36 inch distances on straights but closer on curves, and as little as 18inches on tight radii. Even though the track base is treated wood it will be wise to add a covering of roofing felt to give additional protection from the elements and also grip for any ballast which is to be laid or if no ballast to provide some scenic representation of ballast.

Austrian U-class with passenger stock on a high level track bed.

As can be seen from the previous image, the track bed is supported by longitudinal lengths of wood stringers, which are bolted to spacers this provides the support and stability. Building the base in this manner allows for curves as well as providing lateral stability. When setting vertical posts into the ground make sure that they are firm and will not move this is particularly important on the curves as the ability to form the correct radius for each curves will rely upon the flexibility of the stringers being bent to the radius and bolted tightly to the vertical posts.

The base for the track is now laid on the top of the longitudinal stringers using timber cut to length from decking board, with the un-ribbed side to the track. If running a single track then the cross pieces that form the base are all cut to 6 inches, while this is longer than recommended, it is easier to cut all of the wood at the same size at the same time and also allows some flexibility when laying the track on the base to cater for marginal differences around the layout and at the entrance and exits to curves.

The tops are covered with appropriately coloured roofing felt, which can be left or ballasted to suit your requirements. In either case it would be wise to include a slightly raised strip of material to hold the felt in place and/or to keep the ballast from being washed away over the edge of the base during the rain. The track can now be secured firmly to the base, making sure that the curves and bends meet the required radii from your plan, then the ballast can be added, if desired, however care needs to be taken with the use of ballast as drainage for the track bed will still have to be provided.

Accucraft Groudle Glen Railway "Sea Lion" on Gary Hawes Loudwater Railway.

With the satisfactory building of the track bed, the track can now be laid using brass screws. The track should be fixed every 2-3ft on the straight sections and significantly less distance on curves, depending upon the radius.

None of the methods described for track layouts are completely fool proof, all will need to be prepared and built with care, the greater the time, effort given to the initial build, the better chance you will have of longevity with your permanent way.

Before we finish with track and track bed laying it would be worth briefly touching on the different track types available, this will depend to a certain extent upon what your railway is planned to represent. While this has been discussed previously it is worth revisiting this in the context of track laying etc. The use of 32mm track is typical if you are modelling a 2ft prototype as this is the correct measurement for the scale. Alternatively many modellers now opt for 45mm track as it tends to be more stable and is generally easier to lay. If you are modelling anything larger than a 2ft prototype you will probably choose to use 45mm track, in any case. Track has a code in addition to a scale size and the code refers to the height of the rail in hundredths of an inch - so code 250 for example is 0.250 inches high.

The details on this can be found with the Track Manufacturers Gauge Material & Code Comparison chart.

6. Track Operation

With the track now laid and before you do anything else it would be good to test the track operation. On a large railway it would be worth testing sections of the track, before it is completed, rather than waiting until the entire railway is laid. This will ease the problem of finding any issues by splitting any problems into small usable "chunks" and give you a bit of a fillip. Consequently before you start, give the rail top a good clean, getting rid of all and any dirt or corrosion; while moving around the track section apply small amounts of conductive grease to all of the rail joints/fish plates. Use a bit of physics to help with this, if the grease is applied to the joint and a little heat applied, typically, with a soldering iron or heat gun, it will help the grease melt and flow into all the parts of the joint, when it cools it will revert back to thicker grease. The conductive grease really helps reduce the effects of corrosion and oxidisation of the rail joints produced by the weather, both rain and heat. This corrosion etc. will, over time, cause electrical high resistance or even isolation across the rail joints, these issues can be a real pain to find when the railway has been running for a period. This of course will not be necessary for live steam motive power, however even with live steam a good rail surface is an immense aid to traction.

Alternatively the track can be bonded, using soldered wires, connected across each joint; again this is tedious however it is probably going to provide good power conductivity across the complete track length. Bonding can also be completed by using brass track clamps which are bolted across each joint, while this method is somewhat easier to fit and hence less tedious/time consuming, it is more expensive.

Massoth 19mm Brass Rail Clamps

Thus the type of bonding and whether you carry this out, is really your choice, you may feel that the cost and time is well worth the extra effort for security of future running. One area of note regarding the use of rail clamps; be aware that differing makes of track have slightly differing profiles and some clamps will not necessarily fit all of the differing makes of track, always try to use clamps of the same manufacturer as the rail. Conductive grease is still recommended for use with this type of track bonding. Also note that bonding, either soldered wire joints or the application of conductive grease will require a soldering iron providing a sufficient level of heat; typically 50 – 75 watts would be recommended.

Massoth Brass clamps – ideal for bonding and jumper installation

When bonding take care with points, in particular those with live frogs as these will have differing polarity on the branch rails depending how the points lay, consequently these will need isolators between the rail joints. Likewise with dead frogs, there is a risk of wheels and/or skates causing a short circuit at the frog, consequently due consideration also needs to be given to this issue.

Massoth Insulated Rail Joiners

Before you start to add all of the complications of point control, signalling, lighting etc. on your layout, it is important that you have total confidence in your railway's ability to supply power to your motive power – over the complete layout. Using a meter, check the isolation between the two running rails to confirm that there are not any disastrous short circuits or other issues. A useful help is to acquire a meter which has a bleeper when measuring ohms, this will provide a bleep when a short circuit is apparent. Resistance measurements should only be carried out with no power to the rails. While carrying out this exercise make sure that you also open and close all the various points on the railway one at a time to confirm that these are working correctly. Be aware that if you have a reverse loop on your railway, the very nature of the beast will create a short circuit when measuring with a meter. These will need to be isolated prior to testing for isolation. Likewise, when carrying out the initial tests with temporary DC power, the loops will need to be isolated. With the isolation tests completed it would be well worth the effort, whichever track laying methods you used, to temporarily connect a motive power source to the track, ideally this should be

34

simple DC – the use of DCC at this stage will only add to the complexity and possibly result in multiple failures which is really not advised at this point in the construction.

Use simple crocodile clips to attach your power source to the running rails and then, with the meter, check that at various points around the layout, you have the correct voltage. The exact points are not critical but should be spaced sufficiently apart to give a good representation of power across the complete layout. Note; be conscious of any closed loops which have not yet been fitted with polarity reversal modules (more of this later). If you do have closed loops, then before the power is applied, disconnect one end of the track on the loop to remove any short circuits. You should have been aware of this at the time you checked for isolation, with the meter and also at the initial design stage when you drew the track layout.

Once you are absolutely sure (and if you wish to check again that is fine!), that the power is consistent across your layout, no disconnects or large voltage drops; then now is the time to run one of your locos, it would probably be wise if you use one of the least expensive members of your stud. A smaller model with either a leading pony truck or bogie; or a power bogie in the case of electric or diesel stock would be ideal. The chosen loco should run on basic DC even if it is DCC equipped.

A scene from Dave Lawrence's G Scale Society garden open day, Dry Sandford, Oxfordshire.

Run the loco at very slow speeds initially because invariable there will be some track issues - maybe track joints; track a little out of true, either forward, backwards or transverse. Having sorted out any problems with the track geometry, you can now attempt to run the loco again but this time with rolling stock to make sure of clearances and track coherence across the complete layout. When this is successful you may wish to run a larger more powerful loco with rolling stock. When this works well and consistently - you can leap in the air, shout and whoop; grab a beer while you watch your trains run round your railway! Do enjoy your initial success, you have achieved a lot and deserve to be happy with your work!

At this point you have an operational garden railway and most of the hard work is done, the next stage is to be able to control the railway in the way that suits you.

7. Command & Control

Your track is laid and you have a reasonable confidence that your trains will run around the layout satisfactorily, so now you need to consider how to control your stud of motive power and to manage the operation of your railway services. The initial question has to be what type of control you wish to have and in some respects the answer will be dependent upon the type of motive power you are running. Both live steam & battery powered units would be more representative of the prototypical world if they had some form of control and this conventionally would be radio control. We will discuss these aspects later within this section.

However for electrically powered locomotives there are two significantly different methods of control, in broad terms these can be considered as DC (analogue) and DCC (Digital Command & Control). The use of either will be somewhat dependent upon how you wish to operate your railway, which also will be impacted by the number of loco's, how complex the layout, are you having shunting areas, whether it is mainline or branch line and whatever else you wish to control. In addition costs differences/benefits need to be understood. With a simple single line layout which has maybe a couple of passing loops, the operation of the one "engine in steam" principle, rather than having the complexity of signalling, point control and multiple locos is probably a better plan,

© 2018 Roger Mannion

Geoff Heald's 32mm gauge indoor railway,
under construction - based on the Welsh slate lines

thus a simple DC system would suffice. However with a twin track mainline and branch line layout with sidings, loco shed, turntable etc. multiple locos and signalling to match, then the use of a DCC system would be much more appropriate.

Before moving on to the differing types of control, you will need to think a bit more about your railway wiring and regardless what the source of your traction power is - battery, live steam or electric; if you plan to have any form of remote point, signal or lighting control etc., then some form of auxiliary wiring will be needed. The decision on what is required will be part of your initial planning and design hopefully you will have made provision for auxiliary (if needed) and power cabling when the track laying took place. Cabling can be as complex or as simple as you want your railway to be but nonetheless there are some first principles to be understood and it is important to get it right.

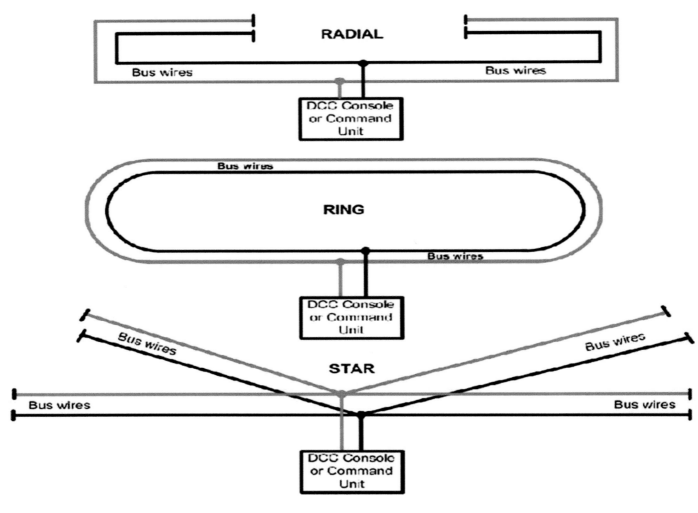

Simple Wiring Diagrams

For electrically powered traction, whatever the outline, you can be pulling significant levels of current along the cables supplying your railway, regardless that the voltages are relatively low. The large steam outline locomotives (typically USA Trains, Big Boy), can draw anything up to 8 amps each, under load or in stall conditions; so with two locos the current can soon add up. Unlike your household mains supply you have a relatively low voltage typically at 20 - 22 volts, so that the work that cables are required to do can be extensive, with a couple of locos drawing 6 amps each and a larger unit drawing 8 amps, this will create nearly 500 watts of power, about half of that used by a kitchen toaster!

Consequently the cable size you used is important, forget the voltage, it is the current drawn which matters, as current increases, so the cable cross section diameter also needs to increase, this is very important for longer cable runs, when impedance losses along the cable will have an effect. Ideally it would be recommended that all motive power cable runs should be of a minimum of 16mm cross section for flexible cables, larger if available. I have discussed problems with garden railway owners when motive power "stutters" at the extreme end of the railway, away from the power source. Investigation showed that in one case, speaker cable was being used to provide the DC power. Likewise also note if you are using _only_ the track connections to carry power then it is very important that rail joints should provide very good connectivity – see above (this should be good practice but is doubly important with higher currents).

Volts	Current	Watts
1	2.5	2.5
6	2.5	15
12	2.5	30
18	2.5	45
24	2.5	60
1	5	5
6	5	30
12	5	60
18	5	90
24	5	120
1	10	10
6	10	60
12	10	120
18	10	180
24	10	240

Effects of Current on Power Consumed

While it may be considered overkill I would also recommend that rather than just relying on the track to transmit power around the railway you provide a "power bus" which can be connected at various points to the track via "droppers", this will be essential in any case if you plan to run only DC systems and have track isolation sections. These decisions will be part of your initial planning and design. The advantage of having a power bus with droppers is that it goes a long way to alleviating problems caused by bad connections between rails joints and difficulties with weather.

Even if you had planned to be a DC only railway it would still be good idea to provide the correct size cables, plus droppers, as this will not only provide a more reliable power source but it will in some respects give a degree of future proofing, it maybe in the future that you decide to go for DCC in which case droppers would be a positive attribute.

I have often been asked about the need for power wiring and droppers, when there is a perfectly good, large length of brass/stainless steel available – namely the track. This of course assumes that a good connection exists, and always will exist, between track joints – in reality this is a highly unlikely scenario unless of course your railway has one single length of track, in which case it is probably, perfectly in order to rely just on the track as a power conductor.

I apologise for going on and on about providing good track conditions, to have good power availability to your motive power, in a reliable and consistent manner but it is important, good track connectivity will save a lot of heart ache and pain. While many locomotives are forgiving of poor track conditions "Murphy's" law says that if a locomotive stops or stutters due to track issues, it will be at the furthest point from your controller; or in a tunnel/cutting! Keeping the track clean is also important, not just of obstacles and the like but also removing the corrosion that will occur in the great outdoors. Remember with electrically powered locomotive stock the only source of power is that small "footprint" of the wheels to track and/or skid. Track dirt and corrosion is a great enemy of garden railways.

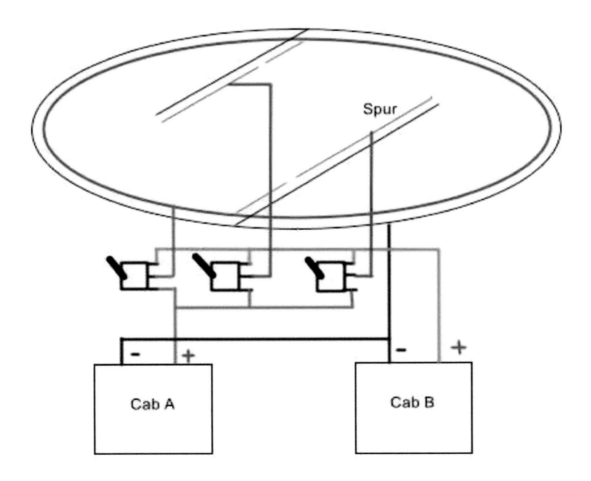

Two separate Cab controllers each isolated by a toggle switch

For your control wiring, signals, points etc., current consumption will not be as high therefore smaller diameter cable can be used, as a recommendation, 4 amp multi-strand equipment wire, with a 2.3mm diameter is ideal. This maybe also considered as a little overkill but remember you really do need to lay your wiring once and then once done you are going to expect it to be there for a good few years. So install the best you can afford; it is important at this stage to get it right first time, rewiring, digging up track bed or cable ducts is not a good idea when the railway is running.

With all supplies, whether power or auxiliaries, it is a good idea to colour code the cable usage so that any future maintenance/repair is simplified, bear in mind that garden railways are by definition large so that when you are running cables and connecting them at the far end of the railway you do need to know what the cable is for, constantly walking back and forth becomes a bore! Colour coding cable helps this – record the coding too for future records; colour against connection type. The wiring size requirement is equally applicable to both DCC and analogue DC control.

The cabling format discussed above refers particularly to electric traction of whatever outline. However clearly with battery power systems you may wish to consider the use of auxiliary cables only, powering things like signals, point motors etc. This is one big advantage of using battery power traction – track power wiring is not needed. However you may feel that to give maximum future flexibility you will install track power anyway, so that if you wish to run a combination of motive power you can. Of course the down sides of using battery powered traction are the limits imposed by the length of time your battery power lasts and the likely requirement for some form of battery carrying vehicle behind the motive power unit.

Live steam traction is also something which will need to be appreciated in terms of motive power for your railway. In this case there is no requirement for power to your track, or if you insist on running both types of traction power on your railway, turn the track power off when running live steam! In normal circumstances you should have no power to the track and the railway will be dedicated to live steam; however you may well have auxiliary power to point motors etc. Of course it is possible to have live steam traction which is fitted with insulated wheel sets to isolate traction from track current. However hot water, steam, heat and hot oils can cause serious damage to electrical systems, if not actually destroying them! Remember live steam traction is what it "says on the tin" - your average live steam locomotive is no respecter of electrical isolation or equipment! More about live steam traction can be found later within this work.

Analogue DC

So what are the differences between the two systems, DC is as it says on the label, a DC voltage which is varied in level and polarity to provide speed & direction to each member of your motive power stud; you can also, by using a separate control panel, manage point and signal control. However only one unit of your motive power stud can be controlled with one controller, for every loco a separate controller will be required. There does not seem to be many multi – loco controllers out there which will deliver the required current, most if not all are single or double controllers, this is likely to be because of the power needed to run the larger scale locos, (more on this later). However it is not unusual to have two or three controllers mounted in a panel plus a wired handset.

With multiple locomotives running on DC only, a very complex wiring system is created on the railway. Not only will separate controllers be needed but also the track will need to be sectioned so that parts of the layout can be isolated dependent upon which locomotive is required to run and where, this clearly limits the number of locomotives running at any one time. With complex layouts the wiring and control systems could be a nightmare!

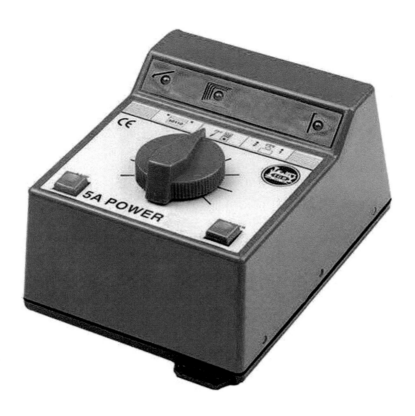

LGB 5 amp DC Controller for G Scale

DC wiring can be quite complex and needs some serious thought and planning – it would be wise, regardless of the type of electrical control, DC or DCC, to add the interconnect design to your original layout plan, again thinking through your ideas and concepts at that early stage will save significant problems when you come to interconnecting your control system after the track is laid. It is also worth noting that different DC power sources are designed in different ways, consequently may not be suitable for all situations. This is particularly true when you convert your railway in the future, to digital control and run decoder fitted traction. (More of which later). Typical of this is the Gaugemaster range of controllers which provides pulse width modulation output – this is good for strictly DC running but must not be used with decoder fitted traction.

The basic principle with DC control is that a controller will supply voltage to all of the track, it follows that any loco on the track supplied by that controller will move in relationship to the control input, this may not be what is planned nor is it particularly prototypical, however it is your railway, so you can run it as you wish. Nonetheless it would be advisable to be able to control each unit of your motive power stud separately. This then means that you need to isolate sections of the layout, so that different DC controllers, can work the motive power in those sections independently of each other. Typically, a layout could have a branch line which is operated autonomously and isolated electrically from the mainline by the use of points, switches and hard wired directly to the second controller. This will allow any loco on the branch to operate separately from the loco on the mainline. The number of separately controlled areas could be increased by the addition of more isolation areas, a shunt yard for example which is either isolated with the entry points or isolation switches, the layout now has 3 separated areas of operation all working independently of each other;

the yard, the branch and the main. This type of layout would require 3 controllers, a separate switch panel for the isolation switches, plus of course the control for the points and signals etc.

Clearly the wiring for this type of layout will start to become very complex and the greater the number of sections which are to be isolated then the more complex will be the wiring, particularly if you wish to limit the number of controllers. In this concept individual controllers will operate a number of different isolated sections dependent upon how the isolation switches are set. Added to the previous complexity is the need for the railway to interact between the different sections; for example when a train wishes to pass from the main onto the branch. Operationally, not only will points need to be changed, but isolation

Track isolated on one rail

Bus cable of sufficient size to carry required current

Toggle switch to isolate track section

Track Droppers

Bus Cables connected via droppers to rest of the track

Simple DC/DCC track Wiring with Isolated "Section"

switches also changed, controllers for the different or incorrect section isolated. Of course that is without any consideration for operating signals! While multiple isolated sections can add significant operational interest in DC, they can also increase the risk of mistakes with possible damage to your expensive motive power and rolling stock. However despite that DC has the advantage of being less expensive and also not needing your motive power to be fitted with decoders but at the same time it will limit the facilities that you can provide on your railway, such as sound integrated with the movement of the loco. There are some good basic sound systems available for DC but they will not have the same range of facilities as DCC equipped stock. Consequently it is really a matter of what you wish your railway to do, how complex you wish your system to be and how far you can extend the budget.

Digital Command & Control

Digital Command & Control (DCC), is a method of controlling your motive power and accessories by "talking" to them. The motive power and accessories are given a discrete digital address, so that they can be identified wherever they are on the railway. Because of this it means that you do not need to have isolation sections and you can run a number of differently addressed locos using the same controller, while also being able to operate any point motors, signals etc., which are suitable fitted with decoders from that controller. There are a number of additional functions which can be controlled on your locos; commanding lights on & off, controlling sound, type of sound, sound function and adding additional devices, typically auto coupling units which can be commanded from the controller. Fundamentally DCC is only limited by the user's imagination and the availability of suitable decoders.

While this is not the forum to provide an in-depth explanation of how DCC software commands the decoders, you do need be aware that there is a basic standard for a core number of commands and functions used by DCC. While there are additional commands outside of this basic set, not all decoder manufacturers provide the same command for the same function; this is particularly true when it comes to sound functions. Nonetheless the National Model Railroad Association (NMRA) has set standards for DCC in the 1990's which were loosely based on the Märklin System; this has since been developed into a core of standard CVs (configuration variables) which are applicable across most of the decoder manufacturers. Nonetheless outside these CVs are a number of others used for different purposes by different manufacturers. Consequently if you intend to programme your decoders then at least a basic understanding of the attributes for different decoder manufacturers is necessary.

LGB Multi-Train System Loco Decoder

LGB Multi-Train System Switch

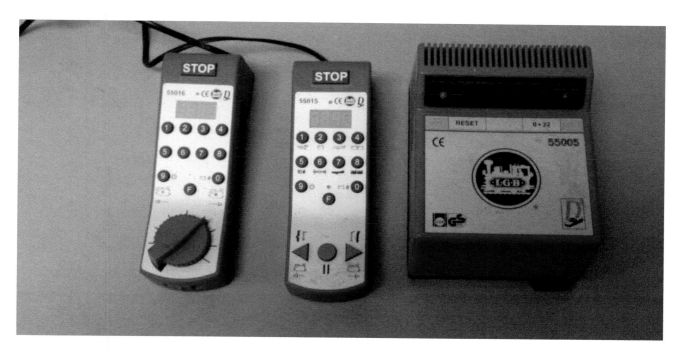

LGB Multi-Train System Central station and Two Cab Controllers

Within the DCC world there are a number of differing systems and these are increasing in number as the ability of DCC systems improves. An early system designed by LGB, the MTS (Multi-Train System), is still in operation on some older motive power however realistically this system should now be considered obsolete. MTS has a limited number of commands and does have some compatibility issues with other DCC systems; in particular it runs on 14 speed steps, using its own control system. (Most other decoder manufacturers, Massoth for example, run their systems with 28/128 speed steps). This presents difficulties because if MTS is run with a 28/128 speed steps systems, certain functions on the MTS decoder will not work correctly, typically the lights! While the buzz word in DCC seems to be compatibility, we are not there yet. If you wish to have sound or other function decoders fitted to your motive power, it would be very worthwhile talking to your friendly DCC engineering team to see what system is compatible and which gives the best sound for you. In some respects the quality and performance of sound decoders is very much a personal decision. However to be fair, modern decoder manufacturers are starting to get their acts together and a good degree of compatibility and interworking is possible.

MTS is now a legacy system which is increasingly becoming incompatible with modern digital systems and is really not recommended. Typically MTS will not run advance decoders effectively or in some cases not at all – this is true where MFX decoders are fitted. Nonetheless there are a significant number of MTS equipped railways out there and if it works for you then enjoy!

Massoth XLS sound decoder and pulse smoke unit fitted to a LGB Engine

So how does this DCC malarkey work? Power is supplied by a Central Station (Massoth or similar) and connected to it will be an operators hand set which effectively is the users interface to the loco and the accessories.

The Central Station provides a constant voltage of 20 – 22 volts to the track on top of which is superimposed a digital signal which can be considered as a form of ac. For the

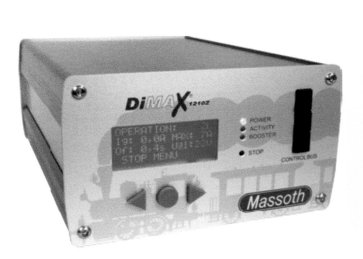

Massoth Central Station

Massoth Navigator

technically minded, the digital signal consists of a sequence of pulse modulated, square wave pulses, where the width and frequency of the square wave (not the level) determines the information commanded, whether it be acceleration, address or function command etc.

Massoth XLS Sound & Loco Decoder

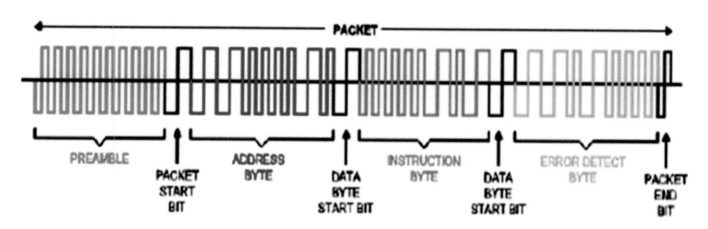

Typical DCC Signal Showing the Packets Used

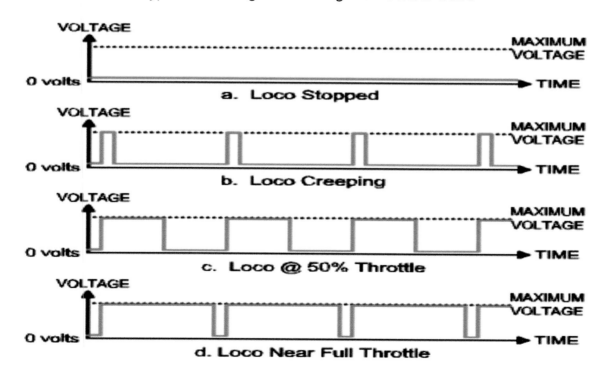

Shows a typical DCC speed change signal.
Note: *it is the pulse width which changes not the voltage level*

DCC can also be used to operate and manage other devices on your railway these could include, but is not limited to, point motors, signals, braking and reversing modules, auto-couplers, smoker units both pulse and standard, lights both on the loco/coaches and on the layout plus of course loco address and sound if a sound decoder is fitted. Digital control is becoming more and more sophisticated with differing manufacturers offering increased facilities and a greater range of devices for digital control. The down side to DCC is first cost, this can be significantly higher than for analogue DC not just because of the higher price of the Central Station and controller but also due to the need to fit your locos with decoders and if you wish to operate the other parts of your railway with DCC control then they will also need to be fitted with the appropriate decoders. However once you have a loco fitted with full sound and a pulsed smoke unit you will recognise the absolute pleasure derived from running a loco which is so close to the prototypical version that the added expense will be well worth the effort.

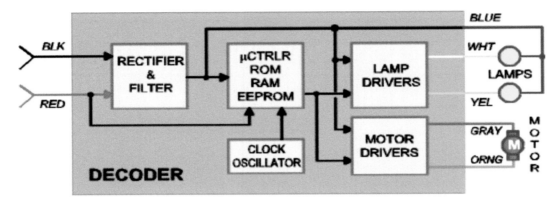

Very Simplified Decoder Diagram

Obviously the decoders whether loco fitted or accessory fitted need to be programmed to match the type of device, whether this is steam, diesel, electric outline or accessory. If the motive power has been brought fully DCC equipped, with sound, then this will already be complete but if a sound decoder is needed to be fitted the sound and programming, it is recommended, should be carried out by your friendly DCC engineering team.

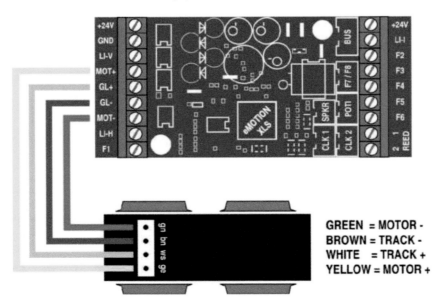

GREEN = MOTOR -
BROWN = TRACK -
WHITE = TRACK +
YELLOW = MOTOR +

Basic Decoder (Massoth XLS) connections to an LGB motor block

Most central command devices can control up to 32 individual locomotives on the same railway, although I would have to say this probably gets beyond the capabilities of most operators and would need a number of extra members of the team, plus associated handsets, the Massoth unit is able to connect 4 separate handsets. Nonetheless the ability of DCC to be able control a significant amount of locos/devices is clear.

Typical Power Clip Complete with Cable

The decision whether to go digital or keep with analogue, is clearly yours and having reviewed, identified the pros & cons, whatever decision you make, the information gained will enable you to be able to end up with the railway operations that you want, performing with the standards you set.

In terms of connecting to the track it is normally better for external connections to use a proprietary connector similar to the LGB device for 45mm track, use a little conductive grease to assist the connections. While some may consider it overkill I do recommend that power to the track is connected at multiple points around the layout. Certainly, either side of every set of points and on turntables, all of the exit/entry tracks should have power applied. You may also wish to have "droppers" in place at regular intervals as well as the connection points already mentioned. Typically a bus cable can be run around the layout and the droppers picked up from the bus. Remember the track and power is going to need to be operational and survive in a wide range of environmental conditions over a significant period of time; track will move through thermal expansion or contraction and tarnish, consequently having numerous power connections will help overcome track power supply problems. A further addition can be the use of cable joining loops – bonding the rail joints across the fish plates thus connecting each section of the rail, this will add to the confidence in connection between each track panel. It is emphasised that these need to be loops as in the change of temperatures the rail will move, so allowance needs to be made for this.

Clearly electrical power to your garden railway could cause problems, not least because of the impact of other uses for the garden; after all it is the area for flowers, lawn, vegetation and pets etc., not designed just for your railway! At ground level track can get trodden on or have machinery driven over it, lawn mowers, strimmer's and if a large enough garden, small tractors. Further, because the supply of electrical current to the track needs to be able to deal with weather and the environment, the outdoors element of electricity is important issue to remember. There is a real need to understand that despite the relatively low voltage, the impact of the current drawn is a very important factor, this can be high, up to 10 amps on some larger railways, consequently, as previously noted, cable types, size and protection have to be an integral part of your railway design.

While I accept most of us will not be running trains in the snow, or a heavy thunderstorm it is still possible to be caught out during an operational session when the heavens open! While electrically powered systems are probably those most commonly used for garden railways, some enthusiasts do not consider that the work involved in building electrical systems to power their railway, with all the attendant problems of weather and environment, warrants the effort involved, nor provides the most satisfactory solution.

There are other methods of power and control, with the most prototypical being live steam. This can be run without any external control system, although this is probably not advisable. Further, if you desire to run models of electric or diesel traction, these can be powered by a "on train" battery supply, in fact battery supply can also of course be used to power any type of electric driven motive power. With both these methods of power provision it is advisable to have some form of control over your traction, even if it is only stop, forward & reverse; else you will be running behind your locomotive attempting to control it. Fine for the 1:1 scale railway where you can sit in the cab but not ideal for your garden layout!

8. Live Steam in the Garden

© 2018 David Goldsworthy

*An early edition Argyle live steamer hauling a goods train
in the garden of Stuart Cakebread.*

A very brief history

One of the great things about garden railways is the variety of interests and the different directions which people take. For some enthusiasts, models of steam engines have to be powered by steam and not electricity. This passion goes back a long way before the First World War when most large scale models were clockwork or steam. By the 1920 and 1930's a number of Gauge 0, Gauge 1 and Gauge 3 garden railways were established. However, many of these early engines would not run well in the great outdoors and were generally only affordable by the well-off. It was not until the 1970's that steam in the garden really took off with Archangel 16mm scale narrow gauge locos on 32mm track and the simple Mamod steam loco. The 1980's saw the rise of Merlin and Roundhouse, who produced narrow gauge steam engines in relatively large numbers for both 32mm and 45mm G scale. Aster produced their first standard gauge Gauge 1 locomotives in the mid 1970's and have continued since then with a wide range of UK and overseas prototypes. A number of manufacturers have come and gone, but Accucraft are now well established in 16mm, G scale and more recently, Gauge 1. An interesting development over the last 10 years has seen a resurgence of Gauge 3 [2 ½" or 64mm gauge]. Very much the scale for the stately home in the early years of the 20th Century, commercial development by Garden Railway Specialists has made this scale much more available with locomotives powered by either electricity or steam.

How to start

Buying a new steam locomotive is a fairly big investment and you need to be sure you are buying wisely. Many people start with a simple gas fired locomotive, such as a geared oscillator from Regner, or a 0-4-0T or 0-6-0T from Roundhouse or Accucraft, which are generic rather than an exact models of prototype locomotives. Your new locomotive will come with a manufacturers certificate of safety for the boiler and gas tank(if fitted). If buying second hand, always insist on a copy of the latest test certificate for the boiler and/or gas tank. The choice of manual or radio control will depend on the design of your line and whether you have a preference for hands off operation. If you then decide you really like steam operation, then you can go for one of the large range of more complex locomotives of a specific prototype. Buying second hand is an option, but can be risky unless (a) you buy it from a reputable dealer or (b) buy it from a friend who will show you how well it runs before you buy it. A number of people have picked up bargains on eBay, but others have ended up with an engine which needs a lot of work to get it to run. Many local groups welcome people who have bought an engine, but not yet built a railway. Here you can get hands-on experience operating your engine, which is far better than reading a book. It's just like the real thing, give it a try!

Railway design and steam

Many people try and fit a lot of railway in their garden and end up with sharp curves and steep gradients. This may be fine for electric propulsion, but can cause a lot of problems with manually operated steam locos. Radio control on the regulator will certainly allow you to operate steam on such lines, but if you want to avoid stress and derailments, then the general rule is to keep both the curves and gradients gentle. If you are only going to run manual locos, then curves of at least 5ft radius and gradients of 1 in 50 [2%] to 1 in 100 [1%] are advisable. Even if you only operate small geared engines, you may want to have visiting locos which may need this more generous trackwork. Gauge 1 and Gauge 3 will require much larger radii of 10ft and over for successful operation of most steam powered mainline locomotives.

You also need to think about accessibility. It is a good idea to have somewhere to prepare and service your locos at a convenient height and, particularly with manual locos, you may need to adjust the regulator on certain parts of the line. Height may be governed by the landscape of your garden and a slope can be a real bonus. If it is not too steep, it allows you to have part of your line scenic at ground level and part raised up for ease of access of operation. If you are operating coal fired locos, then the higher the track the better, backache can be an issue when fiiring!

*Phil Johnson's meths fired Aster, live steam, Gauge 1 loco hauling
a composite rake of visiting BR Mk1 stock on his garden layout,*

A Little Safety

Before you decide to operate your railway with live steam you must consider all of the safety issues, high pressure steam can hurt badly! Typically boiler pressure (Roundhouse Designs) can be 40psi (pounds per square inch), so care is needed. You will also need to be aware of the method of firing the locomotive, the type of fuel, commonly this will be butane or a butane/propane mix, occasionally coal, tablet or meths. In all cases the fuel needed will be described by your locomotive manufacturer and can be supplied by most good garden railway suppliers. Take note of any environmental issues surrounding the fuel you use as some maybe toxic.

Safety and a few do's and don'ts guidelines for operating steam locos.

- Read the manufacturer's instructions thoroughly before you try to run an engine.
- Always take care when filling an engine with gas.
- NEVER do it with the burner lit.
- NEVER do it close to engines that are running nearby.
- Use butane and only use a butane/propane mix if the manufacturer recommends it in cold weather. NEVER use pure propane. Remember gas is heavier than air and so let overfilled gas air off before lighting the engine.
- Always remember to fill the boiler with water BEFORE filling the gas tank. Use clean distilled water if possible.
- Renew the steam oil after every run, drain off the water from the lubricator and refill it with steam oil.

- Check the safety valve lifts at the correct pressure. It may help to lift the spindle with a pair of small pliers to test it is working, but NEVER tamper with the safety valve setting.
- Check that where you are raising steam is safe and does not inconvenience or put others at risk.
- If you use meths fuel, remember that the flame can be almost invisible on a sunny day. Avoid spillages and keep a "squirty" water bottle handy to extinguish any lineside fires.
- Make sure you clear the condensed water from the cylinders before you set off with a train.
- Keep an eye on the pressure gauge, if it drops slowly, then you are running out of fuel. If it drops suddenly, you have run out of water! Turn off the gas immediately or you may damage your engine. Do not refil the boiler until everything cools.
- If you are using radio control make sure your receiver and transmitter batteries are fully charged BEFORE you raise steam.
- Look after your engine. Keep it clean and oiled. Sometimes a light spray of WD40 over the motion and fittings after a run will help keep things in good order.
- If your local club or insurance requires boiler and or steam certificates, make sure your engine is tested by a qualified tester at the required intervals.
- Although steam engines can cause burns and other injury if mishandled, if you treat them well and operate them carefully, you will have a lot of fun.

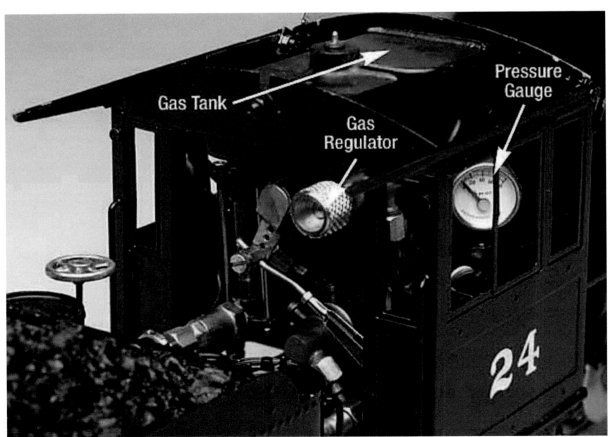

©2018 Kenneth Matticks

Important areas to note on live steam locomotives

How Does Steam Operate

Fuel for the fire

With a steam engine you need a source of heat to boil the water to make steam. Most of the early steam locos were powered by methylated spirits [meths] and this tended to be the fuel of choice for Gauge 1 and 16mm locos. Gas firing was developed commercially in the 1980's and now dominates the 16mm and G scale field. It will be interesting to see if the new gas-fired, commercial 1:32 scale locomotives will have a lasting effect in Gauge 1 where locos are still predominantly meths fired.

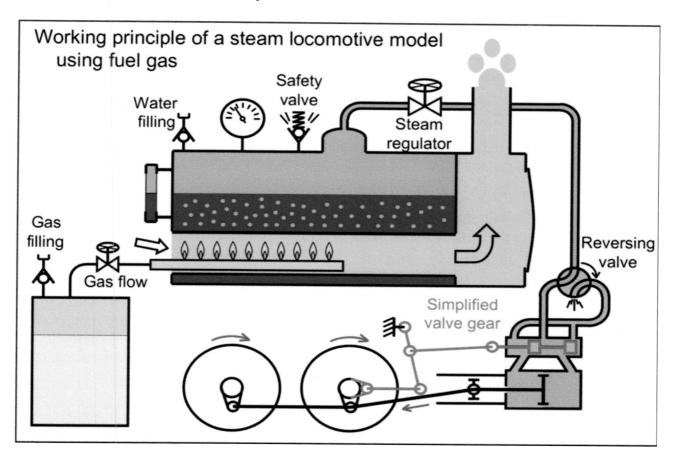

Working principle of a steam locomotive model using fuel gas

Methylated Spirits and bioethanols

These are liquid at room temperature but will vapourise and burn on wicks to produce the heat. The simplest system uses a pot boiler which is heated like a kettle by wicks underneath. This is very reliable, but the flames must be shielded to prevent heat loss. A more complex and realistic system is called internal firing where the draught from the exhaust pulls the hot gases from the wicks through the boiler. You must have a steam blower to keep the fire going when the loco is stationary and need a battery blower for the initial steam raising.

Gas

This is usually butane, or a butane/propane mixture, which is a gas at normal room temperature, but stored at high pressure in a gas tank on the loco. Most gas fired locos in 16mm and G scale have a gas jet which fires into a burner in the centre flue tube in the boiler. This is self-draughting and means that an engine will raise steam from cold and also when stationary. Some newer locomotives have a ceramic burner which is very quiet and efficient.

Coal

This is the ultimate fuel for realism, although common in the large passenger carrying scales, it is rarer in the much smaller 16mm and G scales. The locos are far more complex needing a proper firebox, a fire tube boiler and an axle pump to supply water while the engine is running. Although very satisfying to run, such locos are far more expensive and not recommended for beginners to live steam. If however, you get the steam bug and have more experience, you will certainly get a great thrill from coal firing in such a small scale. Note; to have a hot clean fire it is essential to use hard anthracite for firing.

Water for the steam

The quality of the water used in the boiler is crucial. Use hard water from the tap and you will quickly scale up the boiler and fittings plus likely wreck your engine. People in soft water areas can use it direct from the tap, but many people find it safer to use filtered rainwater. If you are not sure, then buy distilled water. Although it may seem expensive, it is a lot more economical than having your engine overhauled and rebuilt. If you have a source of water from condenser, such as a dehumidifier or tumble drier, you can use this. Many steam locos these days have a water top-up system which means you can add water to the boiler even when the loco is in steam. Most use a modified plastic trigger spray. Make sure you use pure water in this and do not leave it standing around for weeks.

Oil on troubled water

 Steam engines need lubrication. It is fine to use ordinary lubricating oil on the motion and moving parts, but it is NOT suitable for use in a locomotive steam lubricator. You must use a proper steam oil, which is designed to withstand the high temperatures in the steam lines and cylinders; this is available from most of the suppliers.

Valve gear

This can be confusing for the beginner [and sometimes for the expert]. There are a number of ways of reversing a steam locomotive and the simplest is a rotary reversing valve used by locos with oscillating cylinders, such as Mamod or Regner. The Regner engines are geared down to provide much slower and steadier running. Many of the more expensive engines with slide valve cylinders use a scaled-down version of a reversing gear such as Walshaerts. The engine can then be reversed using a manual lever in the cab or remotely by attaching a radio control servo to the reversing rod. A different system is used by Accucraft for their engines with piston valves. Here the reversing lever operates a valve to alter the steam flow to the cylinders and change direction. As with Walshaerts gear, the reversing operation can be radio-controlled using a servo. Some more simple engines use something called slip eccentric reverse. This is operated by gently pushing the engine in the direction you wish it to travel, this sets the gear and you can then open the regulator to set off. It is not possible to use radio control to reverse a slip eccentric locomotive remotely. It can be very reliable and easy to use for running in the same direction, but will not suit you if you want to do a lot of shunting.

Controls of a Roundhouse live steam Alco 3, 2-4-2T

So in a nutshell live steam locomotives can be more expensive than equivalent electrically powered versions and needs more running maintenance, plus there is a slightly increased risk of getting hurt. Against that can be set the real pleasure of running a railway prototypically, including oiling round, stopping for water and fuel; as well as the sound and smell of real steam motive power. We would all admit I think; that there is something special about live steam locos with the smell of steam and oil. Nonetheless one clear advantage with live steam is that dirty track and inclement weather is not going to degrade the locomotives ability to run (apart from rail slip of course), unlike electrically powered track with the rain, snow etc.!

9. Battery Power

If the use of live steam or the installation of electrical wiring is deemed to be too much of a problem than a viable alternative is that of using on-board battery power. On a railway operating steam this could be used, for example, to equip diesel shunters. You would commonly use a van or truck to hold the batteries which would in turn power the locomotive. The locomotive itself would need some modification to operate under battery power.

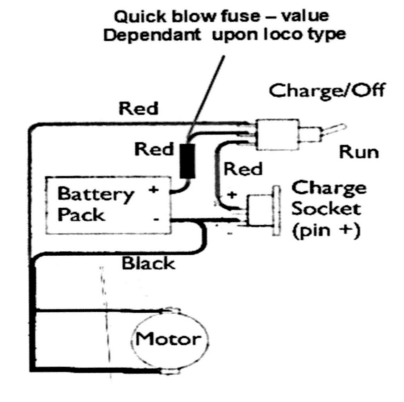

Typical connections for Battery motive power

The locomotive would need to be effectively disconnected, electrically from contact with the track and the motor drive would need to derive power from the battery. Typically this would entail the removal of the track contact skids (if fitted), any wheel/axle pick up brushes and rewiring the motor input to be powered directly from the battery supply, however making sure that the relevant control electronics are still powered, allowing forward, reverse, acceleration, deceleration plus lighting control to take place. A means of connecting the locomotive electrically to the power source in the trailing vehicle will also be required.

In an ideal world the battery power source and the attendant control electronics would be housed within the motive power unit itself. With diesel outline locomotives you stand some chance of having space as the diesel body is, by definition, a form of box shape, allowing some flexibility of fit. Remember that if you wish for full functionality then space for decoders (DCC/Sound), speakers and remote control systems – i.e. radio control as well as the batteries will be needed. The diesel fit is neither straight forward or easy but attempting to fit batteries and control in steam outline motive power can be complex to say the least, particularly in the case of tank locomotives.

The issue really is being able to provide space for the batteries themselves as these tend to be relatively large. Commonly the locomotive motor/s will protrude significantly into the boiler; this of course also applies to LGB motor blocks. Additionally there will be the smoke unit, pulsed or otherwise, within the smoke box plus any electronics and the control/lighting cables being "shoe horned" somewhere inside the available space. With a tender locomotive there is a better chance of achieving battery control, dependent upon the size of the tender there would possibly be space for the battery and the control electronics. In effect the battery would be fitted in a similar manner to having a connected truck or wagon.

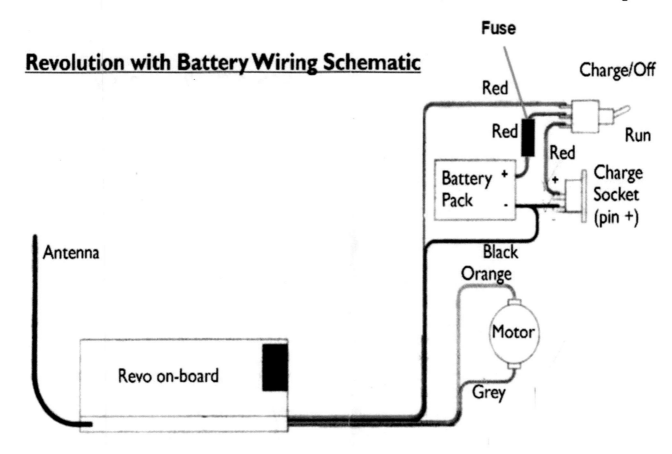

Battery Powered Revolution Wireless System

The system will need a suitable charger for the battery pack. Battery packs are typically in the order of 3000mAh to 5000mAh which means that a locomotive drawing 1.5 amps will run for approximately 2 hours with a 3000mAh battery, obviously as the battery charge falls the locomotive will run slower until it finally stops, although you would expect to have a battery control module which regulates the battery output, significantly lessening this problem. These types of batteries will need to be charged for anything between 5 and 12 hours depending upon the charger and the size of the battery. When you are using many, battery powered locomotives on your railway, it maybe worth considering the use of additional battery vans/trucks, which can be changed with those which are operational, thus extending your running times.

Because of the relatively extended charging time for high powered battery packs, running times can be limited; consequently to extend your pleasure it would be wise to consider having spare battery packs which could be charged ready to replace the depleted batteries. This begs the question about access to the fitted batteries - on a tender steam locomotive, or a battery truck/wagon, it will likely be less of an issue, and possibly also on diesel motive power. However on a tank locomotive, to access the battery pack to change it would be very difficult. Of course a charging port on your motive power, should be fitted, giving charging access to the battery but then that member of your motive power stud could not be run until the battery pack was sufficiently charged.

Added to this remember that any electronic control, functions – smoke, sound, lighting etc., will take current from the battery pack, consequently reducing the overall run time. It is wise when considering batteries to always purchase the best and highest current output you can afford; cheap batteries can end up being a liability.

Clearly for battery powered motive power, a suitable battery charger will be needed, suitable is an important criteria, as the batteries will need to be conditioned to keep them in good order and also to provide longevity of use. A typical charger is the smart charger from Component-Shop – this is designed to charge 10-20 cell NiCad or NiMH battery packs. (12-24V) and has Delta-Peak microprocessor controlled charging, with 500mA charging current. NiMH batteries need to be treated with care; consequently control on a charger is important when using these types of batteries.

© 2018 **Gurdy Electronics Limited**

2.4V-14.4V 500mA-1000mA Smart Charger from Gurdy Electronics

Once you have your motive power fitted with battery power and operational, you can of course just turn them on, set the trains running around your track, however while initially it would be interesting, it would likely soon get boring, hence some form of remote control should be considered and this typically would be Radio Control (RC), allowing at a minimum, the choice of forward, backwards and stop with acceleration/deceleration.

Battery power can solve problems of difficult track wiring and issues with weather etc. but the installation needs thought, careful modification of the motive power and selection of the correct battery packs to meet your operational needs; coupled with a reliable and suitable battery charger. Given that, battery power can provide a great deal of pleasure when running your railway, making your motive power totally independent of track power and problems with dirty or otherwise troublesome rails.

Radio control systems are what it says on the "tin", a radio transmitter sending data to a remote receiver which then carries out the commands given by that data. Typically todays systems operate on a frequency of 2.4 GHz, using Spread Spectrum Technology which means that the transmitter (Tx) and receiver (Rx) are constantly hopping channels to find the best reception at any one time. This channel hopping is occurring at some 1,000 times a second and nominally there are always up to 40 channels at all times, to hop across.

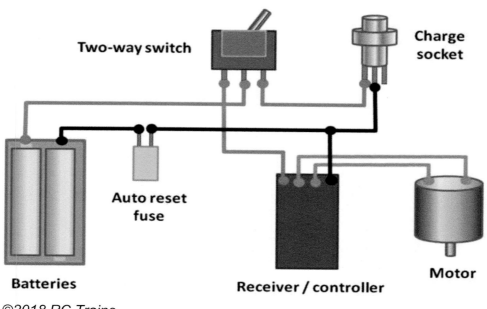

A basic wiring diagram for radio controlled, battery powered locomotives

The older radio control systems (typically 35 MHz) did suffer from interference problems, as well as issues with other operators in close proximity. Because of the better connectivity with the 2.4 GHz system, battery life of the RC unit is longer, nominally some ten times better than earlier systems. Additionally at the higher frequency, because of better availability of the spectrum, the speed and the amount of data transferred is greatly improved, meaning a much more precise and responsive control of your motive power is available. All in all, a significant improvement all round.

I have seen a number of garden railway RC operators using standard 2.4 GHz controllers, the type you see the model aircraft enthusiasts are using. These are good and work well however they are designed to work primarily with aircraft or model boats and have different ergonomic functions which are not always combatable with the locomotives on your railway. In addition they will not always have the control abilities to manage the functions you require, for instance sound functions, auto-couplers, lights, smoke etc. There are on the market a number of RC control systems which are designed for Gauge 1 and G scale locomotives, typical of these are the Revolution, RailBoss4 and Planet series of handsets which give sound and function control as well as speed.

REVOLUTION 57000 2.4GHz Controller and Receiver

This device is designed for scale 1, but is able to work with other scales. The device can control up to 50 individual locomotives, clearly this is the high end specification for RC systems and may not suit all garden railway operators. But again you get what you pay for, so from starting out in this great hobby it is always advisable to get the best you can afford, not just for today but think ahead to future proof your railway as much as possible.

While radio control is a straight forward solution for the control of battery powered locomotives, it can provide similar solutions for control for electric motive power, running analogue DC and can in some cases very nearly match the abilities of DCC, particularly with the more sophisticated systems. Regardless which make of RC controller you use the initial decision needs to be made whether simple handset like the RailBoss4 or one having a full readout display like the Revolution – I tend to favour the latter – the additional costs provides greater flexibility and control. However it is your railway so you use what suits you best.

For the running of live steam motive power, RC has to be considered essential, providing, in simple terms, the ability to control the regulator, forward/reverse gear and on some locomotives also things like whistles and lighting. With live steam powered traction, the last thing you want, is to have to run around chasing your motive power, to make regulator etc., changes, consequently give serious consideration to the use of RC for your live steam stud, it really is not something to be "scared" of. For non DCC controlled motive

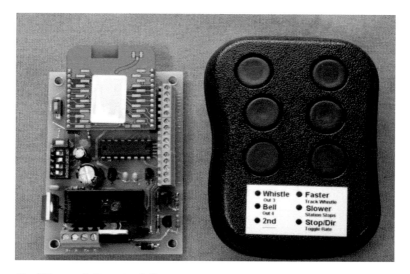

RailBoss4 Control System and Hand Controller

power RC is a useful adjunct to the control of your locomotive stud, whether or not you are going to provide batteries to power your railway, running track power or intend to run prototypically, with live steam.

Wireless Control

Another aspect of radio control is the ability of standard systems to be modified so they work wirelessly, while this is not true RC as is seen with the live steam or battery powered motive power it is a useful addition to providing true remote control. Typical of this type of device is the Massoth device where the standard navigator can be fitted with a radio transmitter/receiver which in turn "talks", via a receiver module, to the central station. In effect the system works exactly the same as the wired devices, without the cables. In this case the system provides gives greater ability to "wander" around your railway without hindrance from trailing cables. The system works exactly the same as a wired system without the cable; it is not suitable for live steam.

Massoth "Wireless" Receiver

10. Infrastructure

What do we consider is the infrastructure for your railway? This can cover a vast variation of additions, including point control, signalling, lighting, stations & buildings, scenery and all the other attributes which enhance and make the railway individualistic and yours. The amount of infrastructure added is very much dependent upon your design and how you see operations are to run on your railway. If you have built a simple single line loop then you are unlikely to need point control and may also feel that signalling would not suit the layout. However if, at the other extreme, you have a dual track layout with stations, goods yards and a branch line you will need to have a significant number of points and if prototypical running is envisaged, a good degree of signalling to match. So infrastructure is as complex or as simple as you wish it to be.

Point Control

While this has been covered in the build stage of the railway it is worth emphasising the need to make sure that points have clear movement so that point blades and stock rails are not obstructed with pieces of ballast or other debris. If your railway is electrically powered from the track it is essential that when the blades move across they make good electrical contact. This can be achieved in a number of ways; droppers, micro switches or solid contact between surfaces.

The first thing to understand is the differing types of points used in garden railways, these are known as live frogs and dead frogs. The frog is the area of the point shaped like a V, where diverging rails meet; consequently it could be possible that a short circuit would occur when a point blade is moved to change the running line direction.

A dead frog gets around the short circuit problem by having a plastic V or maybe a separate metal V that isn't electrically connected to the rest of the track. This makes wiring up the track simple but means that you have a dead spot that may cause short wheelbase locos to stall, this is clearly dependent upon the number and position of the pickups, so consequently may not be a significant problem but nonetheless it is worth noting.

A live frog uses a separate metal V that is electrically connected, but has to be switched to one polarity or the other depending on which way the point is set. This makes the wiring a little more complicated (see below) but of course having an electrically live metal V gives the best contact area for the smaller locos.

In general terms points for garden railway track are normally dead frog which can simplify the wiring for your track both in terms of DCC and analogue however be aware that on some dead frog points, the insulated frogs are not particularly long and consequently with pickup skates it is possible that as the loco crosses these areas, a short circuit will be created. While this will likely be transitory it could cause damage to sensitive control circuits in your locomotive. Test runs, by manually moving your loco through the points and measuring any shorts across the frog with a meter, maybe advisable.

Live frog points- standard wiring

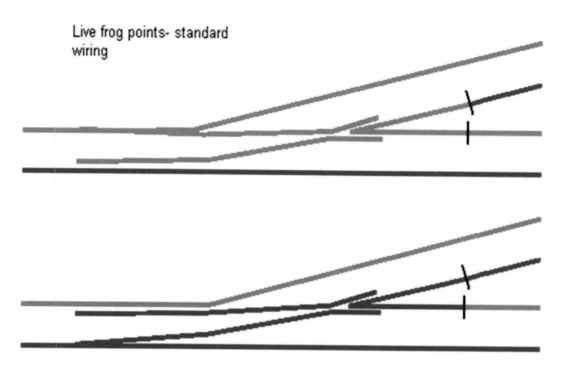

Live Frogs

Arcing can occur here

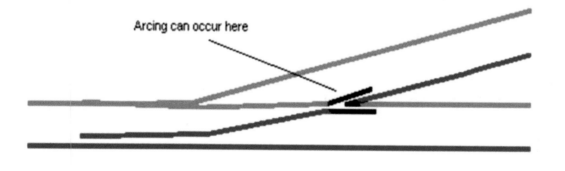

This section is electrically dead until point moved over

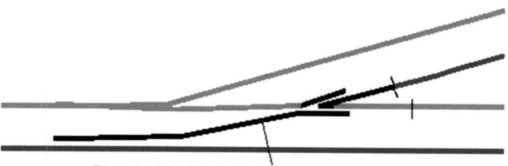

Dead Frogs

65

The use of live frog points can provide for more consistent running through points but does come at a price, the added complications of switching the polarity of the points when a route change takes place, consequently a separate switch for each point is then required. This switch is mechanically linked to the point tie bar and moves with the point. A typical layout of the type of additional wiring required is shown below.

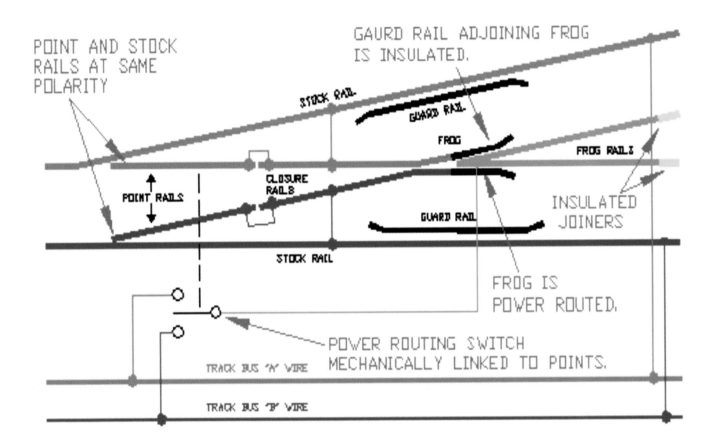

You will note that the frog and associated frog rails are always powered with the polarity of the main line track, the polarity of which will be set by the switch which moves with the point blades. Because of this the frog rails in both directions need to have insulated joiners between them and the rest of the track on the branch and the main line. As previously noted in the track building section of this book, suitable and correctly polarised droppers are recommended to overcome any power issues. You will note with this wiring the problems with pickup skates over lapping both polarities of track power is overcome. Having looked at the wiring of points used on railways with electrical traction power, we now need to examine how the points themselves are moved. Clearly a simple mechanical method can be applied with some form of lever frame, or they can be moved electrically. In the latter case we need to revisit the wiring of the track on your layout.

Installed points fitted with LGB point control

Mechanical systems do exist for changing the direction of the points, typically the "wire in tube" method, commonly used on the smaller scales, however using any form of mechanical system is OK for working over relatively short distances, it is cheap and can be reliable, working well with a small number of points. Modratec is a good example of the mechanical devices which can be used to change points and signals. For those who wish their railway to be prototypical, the Modratec system is ideal as the levers are assembled in a similar manner to the "big" railway; they can be interlocked and also change associated signals as desired. Typically these types of mechanical systems would be used with railways above ground, so that the control system can access points simply. However with larger layouts and a number of points at different positions around your railway, the need for a number of lever frames would be required consequently other methods of control should be thought about.

Normally it would be expected that electrically powered point motors are used to move the points, these can be of the "switch" type when the point is quite literally switched across in one rapid movement – not very prototypical but effective in providing a positive action; or of the creep motor type where the point changes slowly & smoothly, which is very prototypical. In both cases power to drive the motor and the ability to switch that power is a necessity. If running your layout on analogue DC then separate power inputs are needed to each point motor and each point motor input needs to be switched. From this it can be gathered that the wiring will be complex. Of course following earlier advice, the cable laid initially when your railway was being built would have been designed to be sufficient for a complex analogue DC system. Ideally this system will need a switch panel. This could be a "mimic panel" with the layout shown and the switches installed geographically on the panel, relating to the actual point positions on the layout. Indicator lights confirming operation could also be included on the panel. Control panels will be discussed in more detail later.

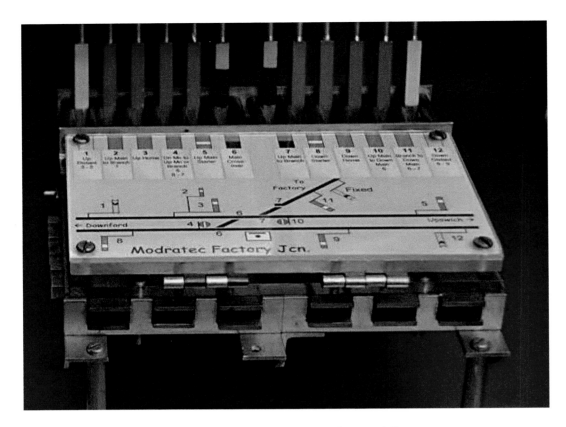

Modratec Point and Signal Control Frame

With a DCC control system, you can of course change points from your controller however to achieve this you will need to have some form of decoder for each individual point motor. This will be either at the control switches or integral to the point motor itself. Each point will have a discrete address which will then mean that they can be managed directly by the DCC system and controlled via the same device that "drives" the motive power; consequently this means that the control voltage to change the points is derived from the track itself. While DCC adds another layer to the system of controlling the points - a decoder - it does mean that your railway wiring is simplified.

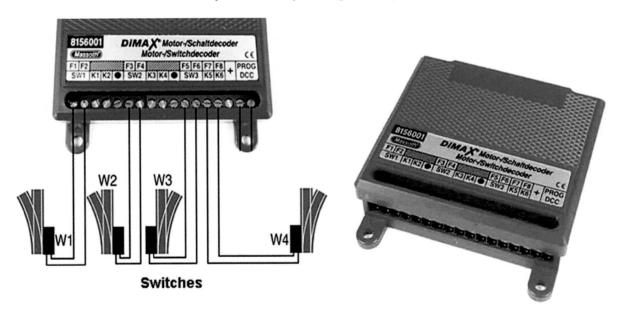

Massoth Point Control Decoders

Signals

Control of points leads nicely onto signals, what they are used for and how they operate. Signals on the full sized railway originally, in the early days controlled changes of routes, which in turn were set by the points. The modern railway systems use signals to provide safety and distance between following trains, as well as route setting. There are basically 2 different types of signal, regardless what outline your railway runs, these are the semaphore or coloured light, the latter normally being the more modern of the two types, although this will depend upon the nationality and type of railway you have.

Technically coloured light signals are the easier of the two to install and operate. This is because of the lack of mechanical interfaces needed, however will they match with the historical period and outline that you wish your railway to run? Semaphore signals whether these are upper or lower quadrant, need a reasonable amount of mechanical installation, to make them operate.

In both cases it is possible to control these devices with either analogue DC or DCC, in the former the wiring will need to be capable of dealing with the additional operation and also have connection to a switching panel similar to the point control. Where signals are controlling route setting it would be feasible to operate them using a micro-switch controlled by the point tie-rod movement, in addition reed switches could set between the rails, controlled by locomotive mounted magnets, to switch the signal motors. This would be applicable with both analogue DC and DCC. Be aware of environmental consideration if adding additional outdoor switching, damp plays havoc with external control systems! Clearly with DCC control the individual signals would need to be addressed from a decoder of some kind and then switched by your controller or handset. Additionally it is possible to control signals, automatically using feedback modules; this does of course add more cost and wiring complications but nevertheless could be considered applicable for your railway. However with the additional amount of control falling upon the handset, it may be considered that regardless whether your railway is operating with analogue DC or DCC, a separate control panel for the signals and/or points could be needed. The decision for having a separate, central control panel; use of feedback modules or simply using the navigator is your choice and will be influenced by the amount of spare capacity you have

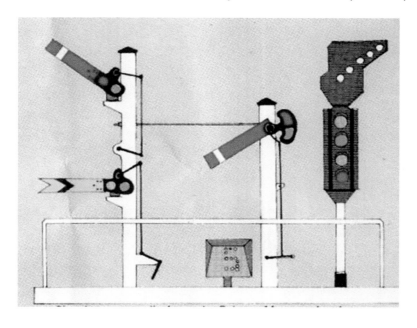

UK Semaphore & Coloured Light Signal with "Feathers"

69

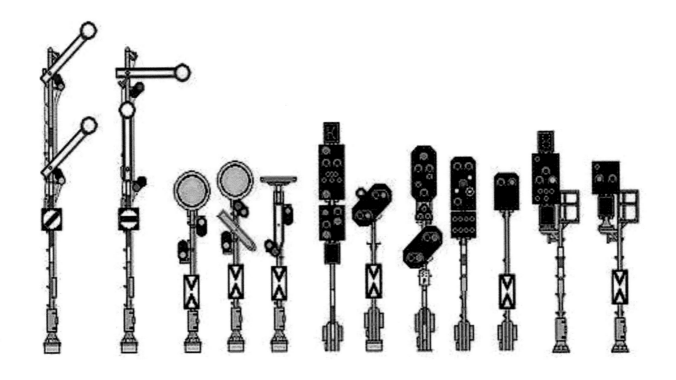

Basic German signal Aspects – both Semaphore and Coloured Light

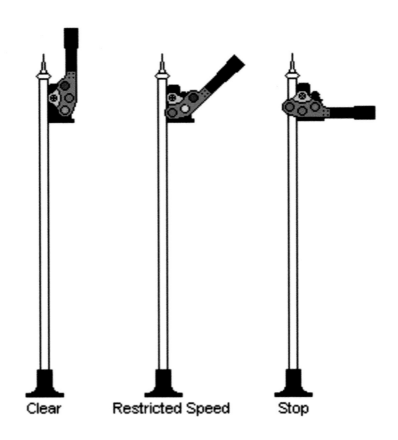

Clear   Restricted Speed   Stop

Basic USA 3 Aspect Semaphore Signals

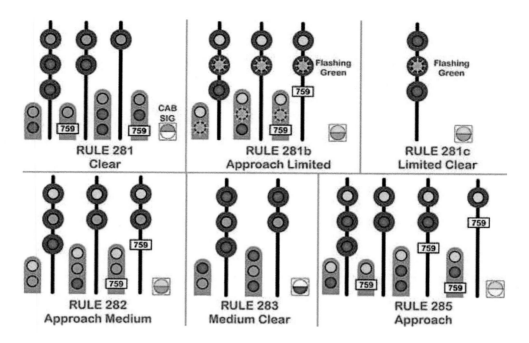

Typical USA Coloured Light Signals

available in your railway wiring and of course whether you included these extra control functions at the very beginning when you planned your railway layout. During the planning stage it would be hoped that you considered any point/signal control that would be needed to meet the demands of the type of layout you were going to build.

In the prototypical world you will find that where there are points, there are signals, in addition signals exist at stations, goods yards and branch lines, where they control entry and exit etc. A quick, pedantic comment re semaphore signals; normally spectacles – the colour lenses on the arms – are, in model form; coloured red and green for home signals, however prototypically the green spectacle is in fact a shade of blue. This is because the signals were originally lit by oil lamps, these gave a yellow-ish light - yellow and blue provide green!

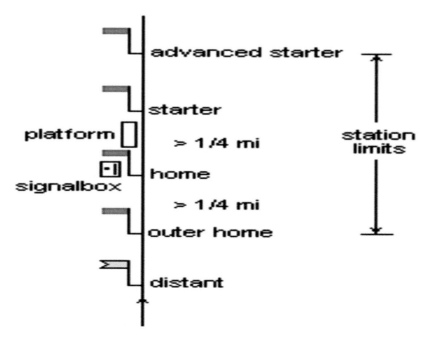

Typical UK Semaphore Signal Layout

71

The diagram above is of typical British outline and would be true for both semaphore and for colour light signals. The fundamental principle regarding railway signalling is that you must not have more than one train, in one section, in one direction at any one time. In very simple terms a section is that between 2 stop signals either colour light or semaphore and in prototypical terms the length of the sections determine how many trains can run on the railway. While the diagram above is typical of those on British railways the principle holds true for European & US systems. However prototypical signalling methods and signal systems are beyond the scope of this book and extensive information regarding the principles of signalling both in the UK, Europe and the USA can be found online and in a number of other works in the market place.

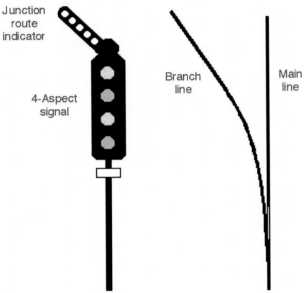

Coloured Light at Junction Showing
LH Divergent Route with "Feathers"

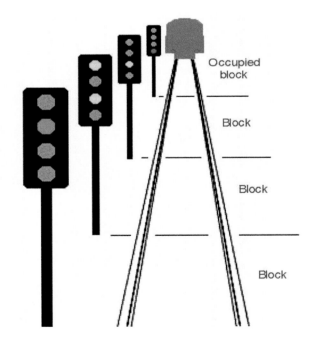

Four Aspect Coloured Light Signal Sequence

If you wish to install a signalling system for your railway than ideally this should be based on the prototype, however as is always noted it is your railway and you can run it as you wish. There are a number of manufacturers of signals both semaphore and colour light all of which can be controlled either by analogue switches with the requisite drive motor or by DCC using an associated decoder.

51910   51920   51940   51950   51960

A Set of LGB G Scale Signals

If you really wish to be smart these can be semi or fully automatic using train detectors, typically those produced by Massoth or LGB, to switch point motors and signals via the relevant decoders; with the Massoth device a feedback module can also be used to inform the central station and/or other control devices on your railway regarding the progress of your motive power.

Massoth Feedback Module   *Massoth Train Detection Module*

With all of these control devices it is worth noting in passing that if you intend to operate your services with live steam motive power, then electrical control of points, signals etc., will have to be wired separately, not using track power; in fact track power and live steam mix is a definite no no! While this would seem to be an obvious statement, it is surprising how many people do forget or lose sight of this. Without over egging the pudding, trying to use track power **and** live steam will create serious problems - track short circuits, decoder damage - not a good idea!

While it is possible to have live steam motive power with insulated wheel sets – there is the additional hazard of boiling water, hot oils and steam etc., you may think that the additional issues are not worth the effort.

11. Control

Once you have grasped the idea of signal and point control there are a host of other areas which can be controlled to give greater authenticity to the prototype. These can be controlled either by switches or by DCC these can include:

> Crossing gates
> Turntables
> Lighting on buildings on some/or all of your railway
> Coach lighting
> Automatic reversing
> Braking

This list is not all that can be controlled; this is only limited by your imagination.

In passing, it is sometimes better to group accessory decoders together, this can be in address terms so that similar sequences of addresses are controlling devices that would work together – points on cross overs etc., or in "geographical terms where devices are physically placed together or near each other, to match the physical constraints of your layout. The hope is that this would have been thought through at the planning stage when the track layout and operational movements are being considered.

Lighting

Lighting is a fairly simple addition but gives a great effect particularly inside buildings and at night. This would normally be controlled from a simple control box and could be wired so that different individual sections of the railway could be controlled for different occasions or times. The inside of a loco works could have machinery lighting, wielding etc. which is switched off at the close of the working day; while stations could have interior and platform lights, these latter on a different switch control. Of course the addition of interior lighting to other buildings and areas on your railway, homes, shops, streets etc. only adds to the authenticity and unique features you can include. With the advent of good quality solar powered devices, you may wish to consider this as a source of power for your scenic lighting. This would be a good solution for the additional cabling for these special effects but also be aware of the limitations of solar power, particularly where the amount of light is constrained by the climate, obviously you will have considered this at the planning stage.

Coach lighting can be controlled by one of the auxiliary outputs on the locomotive fitted decoder, or a coach fitted function decoder; both being switched from your digital controller or could be always on, run from the DC supply. The lighting itself can be "scratch" built or proprietary items such as the Massoth lighting module, in either case the effects created goes far beyond the simple technology used. With the advent of better quality LED devices of both miniature and larger dimensions it does mean that lighting functions can cover almost anything. From buffer stops and signals to bicycles and vehicles.

Railway lighting enhances the railway at night
Dave Lawrence's G Scale Society night time garden open evening

Denver & Rio Grande Clerestory Coach fitted with internal lighting.
Night time running on Dave Lawrence's garden railway

Turntables

Turntables are an interesting addition to a garden railway and can provide an attention-grabbing feature for friends and visitors, particularly if controlled remotely. However they take up valuable real estate space and they can present complex difficulties in design of the control functions. The rotation, stop and start have to be very precise and repeatable to match exit/entry track positions, with the additional problem of how power, along with control, is supplied to the track and the table. There are some pre-assembled tables out there from a limited number of specialist suppliers but these can be expensive. While scratch built versions need significant investment in time, thought and construction. Certainly given the space, a table can be controlled with analogue DC or DCC but by definition each table will be a bespoke design being specific for your railway.

©2018 David Goldsworthy

A GRS kit built 03 diesel on the turntable on the G Scale Society West Midland Group's Maintenance Depot layout

While turntables are a fascinating addition to your railway consideration needs to be given to why operationally you think you need one. If it is only to turn your motive power, and this will normally only be applicable to live steam or steam outline traction, then a triangular section of track with three points maybe seen as a less expensive, or complex method of achieving this. Again as discussed at the very beginning, planning is everything; these types of decisions need to be embraced at the very beginning. I would accept that our railway is never really finished, also that the prototype railway tends to change over time in all types of ways; nevertheless we do need to give time to allow us to enjoy the operation of the railway, rather than having significant additional work, always in progress.

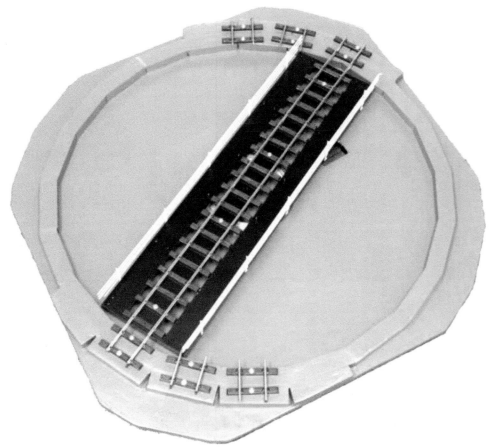

A Garden Railway Specialists Turntable

Consequently having or not having a turntable is an important decision to make, ideally one made at the planning stage. Before leaving this subject having some form of turning device inside the workshop or loco shed could be an advantage, because it is out of sight, off stage if you like, the table can be simple, hand turned with straight forward crocodile clip interconnections. In this way your steam motive power could run into your workshop/store/shed/loco depot, be hand turned and sent out again on it way around your railway for its next duty. As far as visitors etc. are concerned it was all turned if by "magic"! Interestingly, at this time, both the LGB and the Pola turntable are no longer in production however examples can be brought online.

Level Crossings

A further enhancement to the prototypical control of your railway could be the use of operating level crossing gates or barriers. For European and USA outline railways it is easier to provide road crossings as they are barrier protected rather than using gates. Of course this is now predominately true on the modern railways in the UK as well.
There are barrier kits for garden railways, typically those manufactured by LGB. Crossing barriers are a lot easier to mechanise as these only have to raise and lower which is a less complex engineering task. These can be fitted just to add scenic interest or can be fully operational with control provided by a point or signal drive motor, be careful as the LGB type point motor which switches rapidly from one position to the other is not really suitable. The ideal drive would be one that moves slowly from one end to the other, creep motors. These would provide prototypical action for the barriers. The barrier drive can be controlled

via switches as part of a switch panel, reed switches set in the track or by DCC. These can also; with a little ingenuity, have flashing lights which will change with the approach and departure of the train.

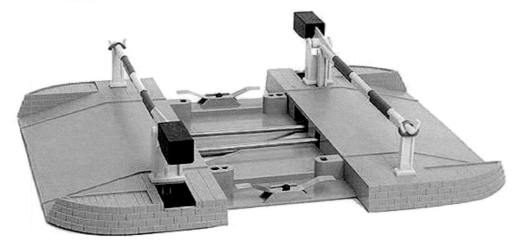

LGB Barrier Crossing

British level crossing gates create a different set of problems, in the first place there does seem to be a limited number of suppliers of prototypical gates to British outline and those that do tend to be limited as to what they do supply. Consequently scratch building would seem to be the best solution to meet the special requirements for your railway. Having said that there are some companies which do supply the gates, for example, without the posts or target discs, typically Penfro Models, in Wales

© 2018 Martino

Level Crossing Gates South Bucks Light Railway

Nonetheless there is still the need to understand how you wish to manage the operation of these gates; there are various options. They can be totally non-operational and only there to add scenic interest; manually operated; or made to operate totally prototypically. In the last case serious consideration needs to be given to the mechanics of opening/closing the gates, including drive and control. Think about how the limits are defined and how they are to be driven. This action can be worked with the use of simple point motors driving individual gates, the limits being defined by the use of cranks and rods cut to match the movement desired. The how and when these gates open/close could be controlled by reed switches within the track operated by approaching motive power and likewise closed when the train has passed. In terminal or end of line areas of your railway, this control could be achieved by individual switches on the control panel or by DCC control, operating with a decoder fitted to the point motor driving the gates. This would probably be more viable a solution in these areas, as the train is likely to have limited room for movement on the approach to the crossing gates, particularly on departure, consequently needing them to be closed prior to the train moving.

The mechanics of these types of gates present some difficulties as the movement of opening and shutting will be different in each area that they are used; hence drive rods and cranks will be significantly different for each site. At the end of the day the additional work to make these types of gates operational maybe considered less than viable but this is your railway so you run it as you wish to. Remember when running accessories by DCC, you will need a decoder for each device or group of devices and these will have an address so that the system can "talk" to each accessory.

Reed Switches

Reed switches are a very useful tool for your railway, the switch itself is pretty much proof against the environment and as long as the connections are properly protected will operate successfully in most conditions. One word of warning, take care during installation of glass reed switches as the wire entry to the glass capsule can sometimes crack if handled roughly and this will let in moisture.

Typical Glass Reed Switch

Reed switches can be a pair of simple contacts enclosed within a small glass tube or encapsulation or can include the more sophisticated hall sensors. Nonetheless, whatever type is used, when they come into proximity of a magnet, the circuit closes and a switched output is created, this will only be the case while the magnet is present, once the magnet

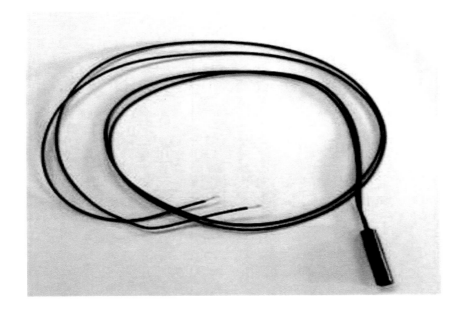

Typical Encapsulated Reed Switch

80

has moved out of range the circuit will open. These types of switches on garden railways are normally seen to be open, which means when a magnet passes over/close to them the switch closes. Some types of switches can be supplied normally closed but the use of these on garden railways is rare. Hall sensors provide a greater degree of control because they are able to vary the output dependent upon the strength of the magnetic field. Regardless of the type of switch used, because the switch can be controlled with an external device then it can be tasked with operating any number of other systems or devices within close proximity to the switch. This could include signals, crossing barriers/gates, lights, sounds etc. Additionally reed switches can be used to control other devices such as relays. Be aware that reed switches are relatively small, and inexpensive, with a limited current draw, normally up to a maximum of 500mA; consequently if you wish to drive a device that requires a greater current, then use the switch to operate a relay which in turn controls the higher current device. The uses for these switches are only limited by your own creativity. Whilst on the subject of reed switches it should also be noted that a number of newer models of motive power are fitted with reed switches, normally under the locomotive. These are designed to allow the locomotive to have an on-board function switched on or off , normally a sound function. Consequently as your locomotive is running on your railway, a magnet could be place between the tracks say on the approach to a crossing and as the train passes the magnet, the horn/whistle or bell would sound and then a further magnet subsequent to the crossing would switch off that function, particularly in the case of the bell! More recent designs will have a factory pre-set time for bells and whistles, hence when the reed starts the sequence the sound will continue for a fixed period. However with the use of DCC this time can be adjusted if required.

Track Mounted Encapsulated Reed Switch

On some makes of steam outline engines, typically USA Trains and Bachmann, reed switches are also used to control the chuff sounds of the engine when a reed switch is set between the driving wheels and activated by axle mounted magnets.

With prototypical operation trains will slow down and stop at stations, the end of the line, stop signals etc. this can be achieved successfully with the use of Braking modules. With these either controlled in analogue DC or DCC mode, it is now possible to have your railway operate in a similar manner. Typically a braking module allows your train to slow down and stop in front of a stop signal, when the signal changes your train will accelerate and depart smoothly. Additionally it is possible, using the braking module, to install slow speed sections, for example if you have a set of complex point work in a goods yard or a tight radius, both of which, prototypically, would need motive power and rolling stock to

LGB Multi-function & Braking Module

slow down and then accelerate afterwards. The braking module is also able to control your train at a station stop and then after a predetermined time allow it to depart.

The braking module can be used in both analogue DC mode and of course with DCC. In the DCC mode the module is able to provide significantly greater amount of flexibility and operational modes. At a basic level using analogue DC control, your train can be made to stop at the appropriate place and then move off; be able to operate in a shuttle mode, when your train upon reaching the end of your line, typically a branch line, will stop for a programmed time, the module will then reverse the voltage polarity and your train will move off in the opposite direction. This could also occur at the other end of your branch so that you have a mainline train stop at the junction, move off and then the branch line service departs for the end of the line, sometime later coming back. All this would be carried out automatically, while you concentrate on your main line operations.

LGB Shuttle Kit 10345

The braking module can also be used with analogue DC control to alleviate the difficulties created by return loops and the risk of short circuits created in such track work. This effectively works by reversing the polarity of the voltage when the train enters the loop, thus stopping the short circuit situation. The use of magnetically controlled switch modules is required in this particular instance; LGB 17100 EPL track contacts are typical of these.

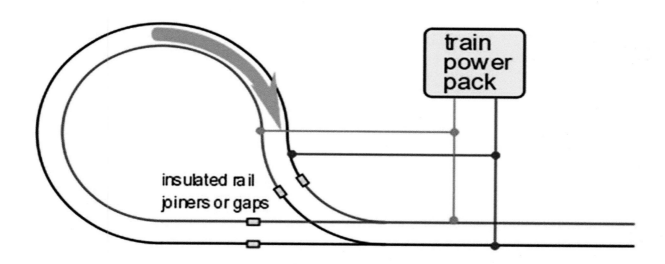

Reversing Loop Showing Polarity Conflicts

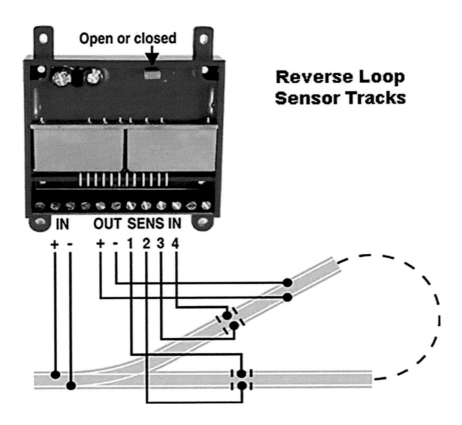

Massoth reverse Loop Module

In DCC mode the braking module is also capable of providing the option of stopping or not stopping when passing in opposite directions and more prototypically stopping when triggered by a signal in one direction but not stopping when returning in the opposite direction and passing the same signal. All in all, this is a very useful module and one which will allow any, of two different functions, to be used simultaneously. Conceivable this could include stopping at a station for a timed period but because the station starting signal had not been pulled off – maybe because another train was crossing from the main line to the branch line – then the train at the station would wait until that signal had been set to off before departing despite the time delay set by the braking module.

I think that it can be clearly seen that the whole question of control on your railway opens up a completely new field of experiences to enhance the potential and operation of the railway. The building blocks are available, as long as you have designed some flexibility during the planning stage then you will be able to produce a railway that will run prototypically; or how you wish it to run and also one that will have as much automation as you desire while at the same time giving you the ability to operate the stock and locomotive stud exactly how you wish to.

Before moving onto the other areas of your railway note that while the modules we have discussed are designed to work outdoors, some care is needed at the beginning of each running season to make sure all is well, insects, humidity, damp and dirt can all take a toll on your electronics consequently it is worth checking everything is in good working order before a running session commences. A little lubricant around the moving parts would not go amiss, this should reduce the incidences of any problems, note the comment "a little" - too much would exasperate any problems.

Despite the ability of the modules to work outside it would be a good idea to protect them from the more extreme weather that we seem to have. Where possible install them inside buildings, under platforms, or protect them with plastic ice cream or similar boxes after each running session.

12. Structures & Scenic Areas

You have got the track laid, the trains are running, you have thought about points and control plus signals, crossings etc. You understand about control and have worked out what level of automation you require, so now it is time to really start making the railway yours by populating your railway with the buildings and the scenic areas you wish to have – these can be as little or as much as you feel is right, can be scratch built or purpose made, built to one scale or outline, be real or imagined, or any mix of all the differences available – however it is built, the choice is totally yours, it is your railway and you can make it what you wish it to be.

Depending upon how big and complex your garden is will really decide on what types of additional features you have on your railway. These features can extend to bridges, water features, cuttings, tunnels, as well as stations and goods yards etc. Now is also the time when you can start to bring everything together, if you have a cutting, what garden planting is required? Installing a bridge, is this to be over a water feature or a lower line, maybe a branch line? Are you planning to have a tunnel, if so length is important and how does this all fit within the garden overall. While it is your railway the layout still has to co-exist with the garden and other users.

Bridges

Bridges can provide a real point of interest on a railway and the structure can be based on the prototypical railway or derived from how your own design matches with how your railway fits within the garden. Clearly to make sense of your landscape and infrastructure these would need to be positioned in an area which can be seen to naturally encourage a bridge, for example over/under a road, over a water feature or railway, consequently to some extent, the bridge design will be determined by the type of feature it is built for.

Bridges can be trestle, girder, brick/stone, arch or wood, the variations and shapes can be almost limitless. Prototypically bridges were built to suit the geographical site they crossed and would be designed to solve the engineering and material availability of the site.

LGB Girder Bridge

As with all structures on your railway bridges can be prototypical or imagined, scratch built or purchased already engineered. However they come to the railway they need to be of sufficient strength to carry the motive power and rolling stock you are running. This will sound obvious but it is surprising how many people will buy a bridge, install it on the railway and the first time the train runs across the bridge, it bends in the middle, albeit not a lot, but sufficient, nonetheless to create problems with track and consequently derail or stop the loco.

SLHCreative -Tan-y-Bwlch Bridge on the Ffestiniog railway

Retrieving your motive power after a failure on a bridge is never the easiest of operations. Consequently make sure that your bridge is secured firmly to the piers at either end, that sufficient overlap at each pier is allowed and if the bridge is of a significant length or required to carry heavy loads, additional support piers are in place, the number will be dependent upon the bridge span, and may be required along the length of the structure.

Smith Pond Junction Railroad Products - USA Trestle Bridge

Bridges can of various versions, including trestles, typical of the USA, although Brunel did build wooden & stone, trestle like bridges on his broad gauge railway in South Devon. Whatever design you install or build will be how you wish it to be and likely based on the outline of your railway.

As noted the superb engineer Isambard Kingdom Brunel was also known to build trestle bridges although not quite in the same manner as the USA Railroad companies. The example shown below was built on the South Devon Railway

Brunel Timber viaduct at Stamber Mill across the River Stow Circa 1854

Tunnels

Tunnel under construction using concrete paving slabs and patio bricks

These additions to your railway add a lot of interest, particularly if your locos have smoke generators, either diesel or steam. Appearing out of the tunnel enveloped in smoke is a sight to behold on any railway but even more so, on yours! Nonetheless to protect against problems tunnels need to be so design as to allow access over the full length of them. This can take the form of a lift out section in the middle or making sure that the tunnel length is no longer than the length of your arm. These design criteria are in case you have to retrieve motive power or rolling stock. You will also need to clean the track and make sure that rail joints are secure and clean. Depending upon the area in which your garden is, you may also suffer from wild life taking refuge in your tunnels, particularly during winter months and the none-running season. When you first run your trains after the winter please make absolutely sure that you have no "stowaways" on any part of your railway. The local hedgehog will not be best pleased if he is rudely awoken by the first train of the new season entering "his" tunnel!

If you plan to merge the tunnel in with the garden and plant over the top, then making sure that you have the ability to retrieve rolling stock and/or motive power, is doubly important. Additionally when building a tunnel designed to be covered by the garden plants/grass etc., you must make sure that the tunnel structure is strong enough to support the weight of the plants and soil plus make sure that it is able to support somebody if they accidentally walk across it. In addition you will also be faced with the threat of drainage, from watering the plants on top of the tunnel, draining into the tunnel with the consequent risk of flooding. So before the tunnel is roofed it would be wise to make sure your tunnel will drain, either with some form of sump which will naturally drain or forming the track base so that water will drain out to either end rather than into the middle of the tunnel. Having water lying inside the tunnel during bad weather or the winter months is not the best of plans! A pool of water is not good but ice would be even worse, particularly when operating with track power - think track shorts!

© 2018 Kevin Strong

*Wood tunnel portal by **VES Enterprises***

In any design where there is serious planting on the top of the tunnel, then the tunnel needs to be built from bricks, concrete blocks or similar material which will not easily rot. This should be set into a firm cement foundation and securely held in place. The roof structure should also be of a material which will carry the loadings and be resistant to rot; typically paving slabs would suit the task. When all the construction is in place and secure, carry out load tests before adding the plants to make sure the structure will carry the weight. Only when you are happy with this apply the soil and vegetation. Regardless how often warnings are given, somebody will, without doubt, walk across the roof, either when redoing that part of the garden or chasing a ball etc. Remember you do not want a tunnel collapse, with or without any train passing though. Repairing/renewing tunnel assemblies after you have completed the entire infrastructure for your railway can turn out to be a real pain and is really not advised. As noted earlier in this work do not forget clearances and heights to allow your stock to pass through the tunnel, it is also unwise to have curves within tunnels, clearances would need to be increased, both width and height, because of this, with the attendant problems of tunnel construction; it would also increase the risks of running problems. If curves need to be included within a tunnel then making the radius as large as possible would be wise. Be aware of "Murphy's Law" – if it is going to go wrong then it will be the most inconvenient place or time and that will likely mean the middle of your tunnel!

Like bridges, tunnels can be of various forms, shapes and construction. Tunnel portals are commercially available to provide a prototypical entry/exit and the tunnel can be an "extended" bridge or a simple wooden cover with buildings or other infrastructure on top. Ideally it should match the scenery of your garden, but it is your railway so you design and install as you want to.

Garden Railway Specialist's Stone Tunnel Portal

Water Features

A lot of us have a water feature of some kind in the garden, whether it is a fish pond, fountain or just a simple feature for the birds. As part of your planning you would have

90

The beauty of all of this additional expense, work and equipment is that you will have a reliable, long lasting, clean water system which does not leak. This will repay the hard work invested by adding a very special area for your railway, particularly with the addition of fish. Nonetheless the subject of water features and ponds in the garden is a complex subject in itself being outside the scope of this work, if you have any issues, it is worth talking to a water feature expert at your friendly garden centre.

A Beautiful Water Mill Feature from Garden Secrets

Cuttings

While on the prototypical railway cuttings are common, it may not be such a good idea to have cuttings on your railway. However the decision will in part depend upon the length of line you have, the space available and the contours of your garden. Nonetheless they do add scenic interest without doubt but forming them can create building difficulties and if there is going to be an operational problem then this is likely to be the place it happens! Further, debris, leaves and stowaways collect there, hedgehogs would find them particularly appealing, particularly over the winter months. You will need to make sure that cutting walls are properly supported to prevent earth slippage; this can either be achieved by supporting structures or by making sure the cutting walls sloop at a sufficient angle to reduce soil/plants sliding onto your railway. If you feel you must have cuttings, and it is your railway after all, then make them short, typically the approach to tunnels etc. with straight track or the largest radius applicable to this part of the system. Clearly cuttings will be part of your early planning.

Rock Faces/Ledges

There are a number of railways where a "rockery" is used to good effect to create that extra piece of scenery for your railway; large rocks can be used to form a prototypical alpine or similar scene. With the addition of stone chippings, gravel etc. a very special area can be created. The use of rocks could include building tunnels, ledges to run the track on or just that scene of special interest.

© 2018 KentKeith

Ledges and Embankments need proper levels - check and re check!

Always make sure that the rocks are secure, do not waste the natural shape of the stone by masking them and try to interlock the shapes to form a natural view and infill with smaller, sympathetically coloured stones and gravel. While the rocks can be secured with cement mortar there is also the alternative of using foam filler provided from a spray can. This is typically the type of foam used by plumbers/builders when filling external holes etc., and can be found in most good DIY shops. While mortar is good for the rockery, you do have to mix it, even if you use a dry pre-mixed bag of mortar and it will be initially (while drying) be affected by the weather, frosts rain etc. The spray foam is not affected so much and is simpler & quicker to apply.

If using foam then the surfaces where the rocks are to be placed, need to be soaked with water before the foam is applied. Once the foam is applied, the rock is placed firmly in place, subsequently the foam, as it gets hard, in affect "glues" the rock in its setting. After hardening any foam overflow can be easily cut off with a hacksaw and if necessary filed/sanded smooth. You can really go to town with this material as it is paintable, so the truly artistic can add toning to the foam. Because it is sprayed from a can you can simply add a touch more if the rock is not quite fixed properly. Using the gravel or rock chippings will hide any sight of the foam joints.

LGB Ballenberg, Steam Rack Locomotive showing gradient and planting

Ledges can also be made from your rockery but make sure that the gradients and the levels, both front to rear and side to side, are correct, meeting the limits for your motive power, plus make sure that the track bed is totally secure. The last thing you need is for the rocks to move, bringing your expensive locomotive and rolling stock tumbling down! This maybe a good place to think about the use of a rack railway, using extreme gradients – these special railways will be looked at further within this work.

The Loco Shed

An essential part of your railway is to have some form of loco shed, workshop or storage area and this should have been included in your railway design. Certainly if nothing else then a dry covered weather protected, area with the facility to store your rolling stock and motive power during the winter months is highly recommended. Unless of course your family are happy for you to bring all of your stock into the spare bedroom or similar! Nonetheless even if this is the case there is still the need for an undercover area which can be used for servicing & repairs – probably the kitchen table would not be ideal!

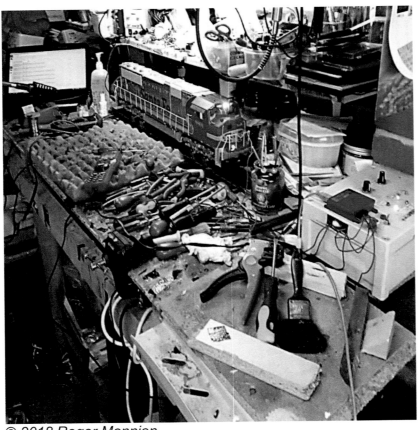

*The Authors Workshop with his Santa Fe SD70 Mac
on the Rolling Road*

Consequently it would be better if a small shed was available which could be fitted out with mains power, allow the ability to carry out maintenance or repairs and could include a bench with associated tools, a test track/rolling road and a cradle to support your locomotive/rolling stock, while work is undertaken. On some railways seen by the author, a spur has been added to the railway which runs off the mainline, through the shed wall, into the workshop, allowing motive power and rolling stock to be brought into the shed for maintenance, similar to the prototypical running sheds. A simple cat flap, of sufficient size will often do the job. The control equipment for your railway would also need to be kept inside the shed and could be hard wired from the shed to the railway via weather resistant interconnections. Remember while point motors, detection modules etc. have a reasonable tolerance to weather conditions and are designed for external operation, central stations, dc controllers etc. are not. However with most good control systems, you would expect to have separate hand held devices either via a long trailing interconnector or by remote radio control. These allow the control station to be protected from the environment while you still wander around your railway with full control. If a simple shed is used to operate and store, remember to add some simple temperature control maybe a small electric heater to protect against frost etc. and if using this style of shed for operating then do move the control equipment back to a warm environment during the winter/cold months, typically the home. The worse killer of electronic control gear is condensation, which will occur in the simple shed environment. Protect your investment!

A loco shed could also be designed to have an outlook on the railway so your motive power could be run from the shed. This could of course include signals, points, crossings, locos etc. being operated from inside your own "control centre". In fact it could become a pleasant "man cave" with the kettle, fridge, heating and railway control all in one place!

Clearly this would need to be planned at the early stages of the railway design but nonetheless it is important that your motive power should be stored securely during any non-running periods. Remember that your motive power is very valuable not just to you but also "attractive" to any miscreants who may have an interest in "borrowing" your stock! Clearly security can be as complex or as simple as you feel necessary, nonetheless it is important to make this part of your planning and costings – it is likely that this will also form a requirement as part of any insurance you may have.

Little People

LGB Passengers plus Guard

One thing that really brings your railway to life is populating it with people, it also personalises it, making it that more of an individual railway which would be different to others. However it is also possible sometimes, to make the situation worse, by using the wrong people in the wrong place or the use of inanimate models.

Preiser Railway Figures

Unfortunately some "little people" can be of the incorrect scale or not providing the impression of life. Sometimes I like to change limb positions of the people, by cutting and re-positioning the arms or legs to a more natural and realistic attitude.

Putting people together in groups also helps, making for a more authentic scene. Adding small dioramas also assists and will improve the effect of real events; maybe the loco crew examining an area of the locomotive, with the station master looking on; track maintenance staff tramping the ballast in a siding or even a passenger talking to the signal man standing on the veranda of his signal box.

© 2018 David Goldsworthy

A diorama from the G Scale Society West Midland Group's
Maintenance Depot

One detail of inhabiting little people on your railway can be the motive power and rolling stock. Normally motive power comes supplied with footplate/cab members but what about coaching stock, cabooses or guards vans – populating these will add to the effect. All these additions will improve the overall impact and add to the realism of the scenes you are trying to create. Extra items, like vehicles, tools and general dressing of the scene can really add to how your railway is seen by visitors. Remember, friends and family can be very critical, so if a small detail of your scenery or diorama stands out and you have to explain why it has been put together that way, then I would suggest that the detail is wrong. Infrastructure and scenery should be designed to bring the visitor into the railway, so, despite knowing it is your garden railway, they believe what they are seeing. This is known as "The Suspension of Disbelief" and sometimes the devil really is in the detail!

13. Planting

Your railway is set in the garden, so clearly plants of varying complexity will form part of it. So the first question has to be; do you want your railway to be in the garden or would you like a garden in your railway? There is an important difference and this is something you will have considered during the initial planning. How you have addressed this question will impact how you plant your railway. We have talked about the additional detail you can add to your railway, buildings, people, detailing etc. and sometimes the garden railway is so well detailed that viewed in a quality photograph, you would have a real problem distinguishing the garden railway from the prototype, no bad thing but very much something the individual has to decide. In this type of creation the planting will need to match the prototype. Thus plants will be of the scale sizes and will be planted to match the types of horticulture you would expect to see on the 1:1 scale railway, in other words planting a "garden" in your railway. There is a further way which is to plant in a manner which enhances rather than becomes totally realistic. This is my approach, it is can be described as the "suspension of disbelief", we have discussed this before but nonetheless it is still valid, basically you are applying your scaled railway into a 1:1 garden, thus your railway is in the garden. However you implement the design and plant your railway, you must never lose sight of the fact that the garden, with its plants, will need regular maintenance, both your railway planting and the garden in general. Consequently plan to allow access and to allow lawns to be cut, plants trimmed, weeding etc. to be carried out.

However you design your railway it is worthwhile remembering that plants grow (hopefully!) and will impact how your railway operates, leaves drop, insects tend to build "nests" or webs, birds/animal life will encroach on your infrastructure, particularly in the winter months and of course vegetation will, if allowed encroach onto the track bed and operating areas, etc., etc. These effects will change as the seasons change and as the railway and planting matures. Try and use low maintenance plants, if possible those with slow growth and of a size which will not "drown" your motive power and rolling stock. Do not also forget that roots also grow, downwards, obvious I know but remember when you plant over tunnels you will need to be aware of this. Having plant roots extending into the tunnel is far from ideal; likely the first indication of this will be the motive power exiting the tunnel trailing lengths of roots! Use a weed membrane and think about the type of plants used over the tunnel roof.

Adding vegetation to your railway is a personal thing and will very much depend upon how you approach the subject. Scale can be seen as an issue regarding plants, but this is really down to your own particular choices, I do sometimes feel that planting with other railways I have seen, tended to overawe the design that the railway is trying to achieve – so take time in considering how it fits together and take advice if and when needed. Review and design as many times as you like but try to plant once - successfully, to meet your railways schemes, ideals and your own desires. Do not forget that it isn't just today when you plant that you are reviewing but more importantly, those years in the future after the vegetation has established. A good idea is to view what others have done, particularly those railways which have been operating for a period of time. This will give you a feel for what works and what doesn't although it doesn't mean you have to copy what others have done, as I have said many times – this is your railway, so you make it so. Another good source of advice is your local garden centre, in particular the larger centres where they have the expertise on site to provide you with ideas of the types of plants suitable. Of course, despite all of the good advice and information you will still have to satisfy your family and friends as they will be sharing the garden with your railway.

A Claptowte Railway goods train trundling around part of Dave Lawrence's
well planned and planted garden railway, Dry Sandford, Oxfordshire

When purchasing plants always review the descriptions, how big they grow, over what timescales and what soil conditions they require, plus the type of area that the plant likes - sunny, shade etc. plus of course watering and feeding can be an issue, particularly those plants which are directly alongside the track, when irrigation could cause problems. A good tip is to keep the plant labels so that you do not forget how to look after them and also to be able to identify those which may fail, so you do not buy them again!

the gradient and that once set they stay that way. The last thing you want on a rack railway is for pantographs on your motive power to get tangled with the overhead catenary when either going up or down the gradient. In addition the requirements for a catenary lead in will also apply to any wiring installed for rack railways.

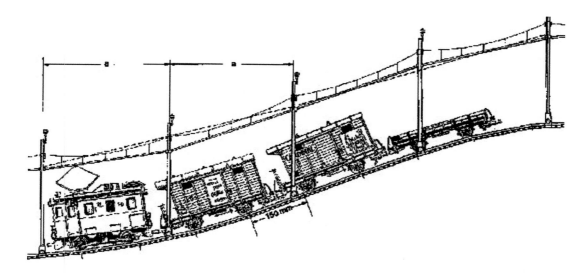

Typical Rack Railway Catenary Installation

Before connecting the power to your overhead wire make absolutely sure that the power is derived from the correct side of the track – simple statement but should be double checked. The internal locomotive wiring isolates power from one rail and takes that power from the catenary; you do not want to have the overhead wire fed from the same rail as the locomotive expects to receive track current from! To check this, place the locomotive on the bench and using your DC power source with a low voltage setting, connect one lead to the pantograph and the other to one of the skids, if the wheels on your locomotive turn then this identifies which rail powers the pantograph and which rail the skid; if the wheels do not move change the connection on the skid to the other side, leaving the pantograph connected, the wheels should now turn. Having identified the correct rail which supplies the pantograph, you can now wire the catenary to that rail. In DC analogue mode this will also prove the polarity of the wiring and hence the direction of travel. If the locomotive is fitted with a DCC decoder then direction of travel is controlled from the decoder input. In addition note that this of course assumes that you have changed the switch on the locomotive, to pantograph power! Finally be aware of insects on the wire, in particular spiders and their webs!

Be very careful when carrying out these checks, use the lowest voltage possible to just move the wheels else damage to the electronics is possible. Ideally it is good to be consistent with the polarity of catenary wiring – it is recommend that the catenary is wired to the positive voltage output from the controller and the motive power, track connection, is to the negative output.

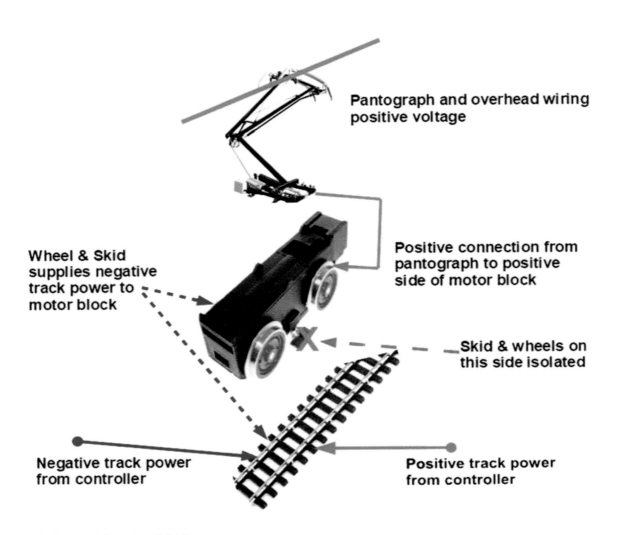

Pantograph and overhead wiring positive voltage

Positive connection from pantograph to positive side of motor block

Wheel & Skid supplies negative track power to motor block

Skid & wheels on this side isolated

Negative track power from controller

Positive track power from controller

© Roger Mannion 2018

Typical Pantograph Connection – LGB Motor Block

112

Coach conversion which would be suitable for interior lighting.
Claptowte Railway – 1st/3rd Coach No 13 based on
a LGB Austrian Zillertalbahn coach

Newer steam outline locomotives are fitted with firebox lighting which again at dusk adds to the overall effect of your steam stud. If your locomotive does not have this fitted they are available from a number of manufacturers – Massoth being but one. They are very straight forward to fit and present a very satisfactory effect particularly at night.

Massoth Firebox Module

Of course some of the newer locomotives now produced include a high degree of additional effects already built in to the locomotive systems. Typical of this new genre of motive power is the LGB Allegra electric railcar, fitted with DCC, with a whole host of functions which can be controlled from your controller. This includes pantographs which can be raised or lowered, significant internal/external lighting including carriage lighting and illuminated destination signs on the side of the coaches. As would be expected there are a full suite of sounds and control functions from this DCC equipped locomotive

The LGB 2225 RhB Class Abe 8/12 Allegra

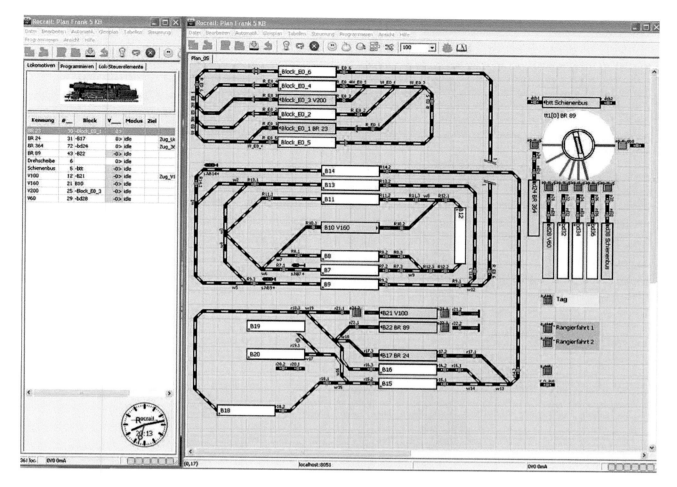

Typical Screen Shot Rocrail Software

Remember with all of these systems, the operating devices, be it your smart phone, tablet, PC etc. are not weather proof and will need to be only used outside when the weather is good or used from inside your workshop, motive power depot or your shed. However this is equally true of most control systems although I suspect that the ability to protect your handset or navigator from the rain is far easier than protecting your PC! And likely less expensive if it goes wrong. With all these systems there are significant control and visual advantages but for them to be at all successful then the operator – you - needs to have a certain level of IT knowledge and be computer savvy!

Märklin Central Station 3

In addition to the software packages a number of manufacturers are producing updated control systems which are providing a greater degree of control and interoperability. Typical of these new controllers is the Märklin Central Station 3 (MCS 3), which effectively is the updated version of the original MCS 2. The MCS 3 behaves as a multi-protocol controller with a high resolution, colour, touch screen, 2 locomotive controllers and a built-in central track diagram system which allows you to build your own track layout onto the controller screen. However this is a little complex and it maybe better, if you wish to control your railway in this manner, to run it from a computer, see above. If you are running MFX compatible, decoder fitted motive power, the MCS 3 will be able to automatically identify your locomotive, this could have some advantages. Nonetheless the performance of the MCS 3 is somewhat limited by the relatively low maximum output current of 5 amps. To be fair, this is probably good enough for smaller railways running a small fleet of motive power units however I suspect that most would find this a restriction, particularly if running the bigger USA outline locomotives. Märklin do provide booster units which can be added to the MCS 3 however these are also limited to 5 amps and to provide additional power need to be connected to separate, isolated sections, adding complications to your wiring.

LokSound 5 DCC Decoder

At the time of publication, (2019), Märklin do not provide G Scale decoders, so to use the Märklin system will need you to run your motive power using MFX compatible decoders, typically the ESU LokSound V5. With existing legacy motive power, if running on Märklin CS2/3 control systems, it is recommended that you check that existing digital systems are compatible. CS2/3 systems are able to run DCC protocol but legacy systems will not be able to take full advantage of all of the Märklin capabilities.

Be aware that more manufacturers are tending to move towards propriety systems which are not always operational with all other manufacturers. Nevertheless the choice of control system is entirely yours; it is your railway and you can power and run it how you wish!

19. Now Go & Enjoy!

From this grand idea of a railway in the garden to enjoy and share; you have sat down, researched and planned how it should look and work. You have strained your back building, digging and laying the ground work; you have dug the holes in the garden; wired the power cables with the correct size cables. Watched and enjoyed the pleasure as the railway grew, became established and was shaped to your railway in the garden. Decisions have been made regarding what the outline of the motive power should be; what power source - live steam, battery or track powered. You have decided whether control should be analogue or DCC, chosen your system and the controller. The track is laid, bridges and tunnels built, the plants are growing and look stunning. The buildings are up, the little people inhabit your railway and services are running as you visualised.

Congratulations; you and your railway have come a long way, sit back with your chosen tipple feel the warmth on your back and enjoy as your trains perform, the way you want them to - on your railway!

I am not needed anymore!

20. Appendices

Appendix 1

Plants for the Railway

This is not a definitive list, nor that recommended only those which I have seen work, in the right soil and conditions.

Erica x Darleyensis Kramers Red
Erica Arborea "Alberts Gold"
Hebes
Green Globe
Sclerathus Uniflorus
Archer's Gold
Alpines
Cyclamen
Lonicera Nitida
Mini Conifers
Chamaecyparis Lawsoniana,
Arenaria Caespitosa
Saxifrage
Sedum Hispanicum Glaucum
Soleirolia Soleirolii
Campanula
Sedum Spathulifolium

Plants recommended or used by others:

This is a list used by others not by the author, but which seem to work in the right soil and conditions.

Ground cover

Arenaria balearica (sandwort)
Calluna vulgaris Foxii Nana (a tiny heather)
Frankenia laevis (bit invasive)
Mentha requiennii
Minuartia imbricato (invasive)
Potentilla eriocarpa
Raoulia (australis, glabra, lutescens) hard to grow good drainage required
Sagina boydii
Scleranthus biflorus (ideal miniature grass)
Soleirolia solerolii invasive
Viola yakusimana (a tiny violet)

Shrubs

Arcterica nana (likes some shade)
Berberis Corallina Compacta (like a tiny holly bush)
Cotoneaster congestus nanus
Genista sagittalis pilosa minor (mini gorse)
Jasminum parkeri (mini jasmine slightly tender)

Rhododendron radicans (grows to only 4 inches)
Rubus articus (mini bramble largish leaves can be invasive)
Thymus Doone Valley (looks like mini golden privet)
Tsusiophyllum tanakae (tiny formal shrub needs shade and peat)
Evergreen tree
Lonicera nitida

Deciduous trees

Betula nana (mini birch tree)
Salix boydii (easy to grow)
Salix herbacea (creeping willow)
Salix hylematica
Salix myrsinites (mini weeping willow)
Salix retusa
Sorbus reducta (mini mountain ash)
Syringa velutina (palibiniana) [mini lilac]
Ulmus parvifolia (tiny elm)

Conifers

Abies balsamea hudsonia
Chamaecyparis obtusa nana caespitosa (very small and slow growing)
Chameacyparis pisifera nana
Crytomeria japonica vilmoriniana (like a mini monkey puzzle tree)
Juniperus communis compressa (like a mini Lombardy poplar)
Juniperus coxii (weeping poplar)
Picea abies pygmaea
Picea mariana nana
Thuja orientalis minima

General

Acaena Buchananii
Thyme, Bressingham Pink
Thymus minimus
Varius Sedums
Saxifrages
Juniper compressa
Picea Albertina Conica

Appendix 2

Controllers Supported By:

Freiwald Train Controller Software

CAN-digital-Bahn CC-Schnitte
CAN-digital-Bahn PC-Schnitte
CTI
D&H / MTTM Future-Central-Control
DiCoStation by Littfinski Daten Technik
Digitrax LocoNet
Dinamo
EasyDCC
Edits
ESU ECoS
ESU Navigator
Fleischmann (Z21, z21, multiZENTRALEpro 686702, Twin Center, FMZ)
HELMO Inter-10 and Inter-1
Hornby
HSI-88 by Littfinski DatenTechnik
Lenz Digital Plus (all Interfaces)
Lionel TrainMaster
Märklin Central Station 1, 2, 3
Maerklin Digital (Central Unit 602x with Interface 6050/6051)
Massoth
MegaDecoder
MoBaSBS
Muet Digirail (incl. train identification with MUET 8i)
Rautenhaus Digital (RMX and SLX)
NCE Power Pro
RCI by Oak Tree Systems (incl. support of analog locomotives without own decoder)
Roco (Z21, z21, Multizentrale 10832/10786 and Rocomotion-Interface 10785)
SPROG
Stärz ZS1, ZS2 and Bus-Interface
Tams EasyControl
Tams RC-Link
TracTronics SECSI
Tran CT Elektronik
Trix Selectrix Interface 66824 and 66842
Uhlenbrock Intellibox (Intellibox I and II, IB-COM and IB-Basic)
Zimo
ZTC
µCon S88-Master

Appendix 3

Controllers Supported By:

Rocrail Software Systems

bidib	http://www.bidib.org
cbus	http://www.merg.org.uk/resources/lcb.html
cti	http://www.cti-electronics.com/
ddx	DDX
dcc232	DCC232
dccpp	DCC++
dccar	PC Sender
dinamo	Dinamo v3.0
dmx4all	DMX4ALL USB interface
dmxartnet	AVR-ArtNetNode
dmxeurolite	EutoLite USB-DMX512-Pro
easydcc	CVP Products
ecos	ECoS Controller (ESU Website), Märklin Central Station 1 Reloaded (ESU Website)
editspro	
esunavi	ESU Navigator
got	
hue	
hsi88	LDT website LDT website USB PC-Schnitte
Infracar	
lcm	
loconet	Digitrax LocoNet LocoBuffer, LocoBuffer-USB, IntelliBox Basic I/II, IB-Com, LbServer, DR5000.
mcs2/3	Märklin Central Station 2/3 (Märklin Website)
massoth	Massoth DiMAX
mdrrc	Model Digital Railroad Central Station
mttmfcc	MTTM FCC
muet	Müt MC2004
nce	NCE DCC
om32	Dinamo OM32/OC32 RS485
opendcc	OpenDCC
p50	Märklin 6050/51
p50x	IntelliBox (TWIN-Center, OpenDCC, Tams,MrDirect, DIGITAL-S-INSIDE, MDRRC)
perir	Per's Model Train recognition system
rclink	Tams RailCom Link
raptor	Raptor Digital
rfid12	MERG Kits
rmx	Rautenhaus
rocnet	Open Rocrail Protocol
roco	Roco 10785
rocomp	MultiZentralePro

tamsmc	Tams
slx	SLX825, Stärz ZS1
spl	Elektor
sprog	SPROG II
srcp	Simple Railroad Command Protocol
µCon-S88	S88 Bus master.
virtual	Virtual test CS
xpressnet	Lenz LI100/LI100F, LI101, LI-USB, OpenDCC, Hornby Elite, Atlas Commander, GenLi, Viessmann Commander, DR5000
zimo	Zimo MX1
zimobin	Zimo MX1, MX1EC
zimocan	Zimo MX10
zs2	ZS2
z21/Z21	Z21

Appendix 4

Typical Tools for Your Railway

This list is not exhaustive and you can probably manage with less to start with, but all will be used at some time and you will rue the day you have not got the right tool!

Variable Temperature Soldering Iron
Solder Pump
Small Bench Vice
LED Torches (X2 at least)
Head Torch (recommended)
A Good Quality Third Hand, with Glass
A Good Quality, Lit, Hands Free Magnifier or OptiVISOR®, with Light (recommended)
Decent Set of Good Tweezers
Hot Glue Gun
Hot Air Gun (for heat shrink tube)
Volt, Amp, Ohm Meter (recommended that it has a continuity bleeper)
Set of BA Nut Spinners
Set of Small Metric Sockets
Set of Needle Files
Set of Jewellers Screw Drivers
Complete Set of Cross Head Screw Drivers
Complete Set of Philips Screw Drivers
Set of Flat bladed Screw Drivers
Medium Head, Long Shaft Philips Screw Driver
Medium Head Long Shaft Flat Blade Screw Driver
Razor Saw
Glass Fibre Brush
Good Quality Stanley Knife & Set of Scalpels
Pot Conductive Grease (for track joints)
Pin Hammer
Automatic Wire Strippers (recommended)
Small Adjustable Spanner
Small, Computer Tool Kit (to include small long nose plyers & side cutters)
Track Cleaning Pad
Magnet (for testing track and motive power reed switches)
Small Wire Brush
Sundry Paint Brushes
Lubricating Oil, Gear Oil, Light Gear Grease (as appropriate)
Rollers to form Rolling Road (6 minimum – ideally 8)
Steam Oil (If appropriate)
Notebook (for that detail you will forget if not written down at the time!)

Appendix 5

Decoder Differences

MTS I

The oldest decoder protocol – has 14 speed steps only, no switches, only 8 addresses and serial only commands. This means that control commands are slower and there is a wait period for different commands to be actioned because the information blocks appear at the decoder one after another. Serial commands mean that commands happen one after another. Parallel means that more than one command can occur simultaneously.

MTS II,

14 speed steps only, but with additional addresses, now 22, although this is still a serial command system.

MTS II with P for parallel.

This is similar to MTS II, having 22 addresses and 14 speed steps but the protocol now runs a parallel command system, allowing faster information and providing for greater data transfer.

MTS III the latest being sold.

14 speed steps only and up to 23 loco addresses however if connected to the Massoth DiMAX navigator up to 10,239 addresses can be used and 28 speed steps applied.

Note:
All of the above decoder types are legacy design and will only run to a maximum power consumption of 5 amps. To improve on this a separate booster pack for use on a second isolated section of track, which could complicate the wiring for your railway. There are limitations with the MTS system - nonetheless it has been used successfully for some time and has proved to be popular. Nonetheless these systems are now of limited availability and will not run successfully with CS2/CS3 systems and advance decoders.

Massoth

The Massoth system does have 128 speed steps, short and long addressing (9,999 addresses), plus can provide decoders that will work up to 10 amps peak current.
Zimo

The Zimo system provides up to 128 speed steps, short & long addressing and up to 10 amp peak current. Zimo decoders support JMRI.

Märklin CS 2/CS 3 Control Systems

The associated decoders for the Märklin system support 128 speed steps and long/short addressing but are limited to 5 amp peak current provided by the CS control system, they are equipped to provide up to 32 switch functions. Nonetheless large scale railways will need to use MFX compatible decoders.

ESU

The Loksound series of decoders from ESU have recently been upgraded – the new v5 devices are now capable of providing 32 switch functions and can also automatically log onto the Märklin CS systems, as well being described as a true multi – protocol decoder.

Appendix 6

Scale and Track Gauge - A Simple Comparison

Although certain scales are marked as either USA or UK, this is not a strict split of usage and in practice, both versions are found all over the world. These have been designated in this way to indicate the more commonly usage. There are also a number of different sub divisions within the various gauges: typically fine-scale or standard etc. these relate mainly to track and wheel standards.

0 gauge is included as this is the smallest that can sensibly be used outdoors; nonetheless they are not in common use.

> ### Gauge '0' (UK)
> 7mm :1 foot scale (1:43.5) - running on 32mm gauge track. Models are of standard gauge railways.

> ### Gauge '0' (USA)
> 1/4":1 foot scale (1:48) running on 32mm gauge track. Models are of standard gauge railways.

> ### Gauge '1' (USA)
> 3/8":1 foot (1:32) running on 45mm gauge track. Models are of standard gauge railways.

> ### Gauge '1'(UK)
> 10mm :1 foot scale (1:30.5) running on 45mm gauge track. Models are of standard gauge railways.

> ### 1/2" scale (USA)
> 1/2":1 foot (1:24) running on 45mm gauge track. Models are of narrow gauge railways.

> ### 'G' scale
> 13.5mm :1 foot (1:22.5) running on 45mm gauge track. Models are of narrow gauge railways. NOTE, Some models described simply as 'G' scale are actually built to 1:20.3 to represent 3 foot gauge equipment; Typically LGB, Bachmann etc.

> ### 5/8" scale (USA)
> 5/8":1 foot (1:19.2) running on 45mm gauge track. Models are of narrow gauge railways.

> ### SM32
> 16mm :1 foot scale (1:19) running on 32mm gauge track. Models are of narrow gauge railways.

> ### SM45
> 16mm :1 foot scale (1:19) running on 45mm gauge track. Models are of narrow gauge railways.

➤ 7/8N2 (USA)

7/8":1 foot scale (1:13.7) running on 45mm gauge track. Models are of narrow gauge railways and represent 2 foot gauge.

Garden railway scales and gauges

A little extra information is added for what are generally termed the Garden Railway scales as there are several which are normally used together and can cause confusion. Although any railway laid round a garden can be called a garden railway, today the term is normally applied to Gauge 1, 'G' scale, SM32 and SM45.

'G' scale, SM32 and SM45 are normally grouped together as size compatible, despite the scales being slightly different. Though we have two different gauges, 32 and 45mm, all three represent narrow gauge models and have similar overall sizes of locomotives and stock.

Appendix 7
National Model Railroad Association (NMRA)
Standard Configuration Variables (CV's)

Table 1 Multi-function Decoder Configuration Variables

CV Name	CV #	Required	Default Value	Read Only	Uniform Spec	Dynamic (Volatile)	Additional Comments
Multi-function Decoders:							
Primary Address	1	M	3		Y		
Vstart	2	R					
Acceleration Rate	3	R					
Deceleration Rate	4	R					
Vhigh	5	O					
Vmid	6	O					
Manufacturer Version No.	7	M		Y			Manufacturer defined version info
Manufactured ID	8	M		Y	Y		Values assigned by NMRA
Total PWM Period	9	O					
EMF Feedback Cutout	10	O					
Packet Time-Out Value	11	R					
Power Source Conversion	12	O			Y		Values assigned by NMRA
Alternate Mode Function Status F1-F8	13	O			Y		
Alternate Mode Function. Status F$_L$,F9-F12	14	O			Y		
Decoder Lock	15-16	O			Y		
Extended Address	17+18	O			Y		
Consist Address	19	O			Y		
	20	-					Reserved by NMRA for future use
Consist Addr Active for F1-F8	21	O			Y		
Consist Addr Active for FL-F9-F12	22	O			Y		
Acceleration Adjustment	23	O			Y		
Deceleration Adjustment	24	O			Y		
Speed Table/Mid-range Cab Speed Step	25	O			Y		
	26						Reserved by NMRA for future use
Decoder Automatic Stopping Configuration	27	O			Y		Under re-evaluation – see details
Bi-Directional Communication Configuration	28	O			Y		Under re-evaluation – see details
Configuration Data #1	29	M[1]			Y		
Error Information	30	O			Y		
Index High Byte	31	O			Y		Primary index for CV257-512 00000000 - 00001111 reserved by NMRA for future use.
Index Low Byte	32	O			Y		Secondary index for CV257-512
Output Loc. FL(f), FL(r), F1-F12	33-46	O			Y		
Manufacturer Unique	47-64	O					Reserved for manufacturer use
Kick Start	65	O					
Forward Trim	66	O					
Speed Table	67-94	O					
Reverse Trim	95	O					
	96-104	-					Reserved by NMRA for future use
User Identifier #1	105	O					Reserved for customer use
User Identifier #2	106	O					Reserved for customer use
	107-111	-					Reserved by NMRA for future use CV107,108: expanded Mfg. ID CV109-111: expanded CV7
Manufacturer Unique	112-256	O					Reserved for manufacturer use
Indexed area	257-512						Indexed area - see CV# 31,32 Index values of 0-4095 reserved by NMRA
	513-879	-					Reserved by NMRA for future use
	880-891					Y	Reserved by NMRA for future use
Decoder Load	892	O			Y	Y	
Dynamic Flags	893	O			Y	Y	
Fuel/Coal	894	O			Y	Y	
Water	895	O			Y	Y	
SUSI Sound and Function Modules	896-1024	O			Y		See TN-9.2.3

The NRMA has over a number of years formulated a number of standards for garden railway systems and while they are an independent US organisation, their standards have become accepted, by & large, across the hobby by all manufacturers.

The CV table shows the core block of common CV's which are used for the same function by all manufacturers, however be aware that some CV numbers which do not form the core block, will have different control functions dependent upon the decoder manufacturer – so do not assume that a function output for a given CV will be the same for the same CV number with a different manufacturer – always check!

Appendix 8.

A Selection of Relevant Magazines
This list is not exhaustive.

Garden Rail – UK Magazine

Garden Railways – Also UK based.

Railway Magazine – Useful Prototype information

Railway Modeller – mostly smaller scales but sometimes has good garden railway information.

British Railway Modelling – again mostly the smaller scales but occasional large scale details.

Gartenbahn Profi Magazine – German language but English Translations available

Steam in the Garden – North American publication for garden railroad steam

NMRA Magazine – House magazine of the NRMA

O Gauge Railroading – US 0 gauge magazine

Narrow Gauge & Shortline Gazette – Publication for those interested in narrow gauge Systems

Continental Modeller – examines the world scene but mostly at the smaller scales.

Australian Model Engineering Magazine - Australian based provides both prototype and modelling information, mainly large-scale live steam.

Appendix 9

Clubs and Societies of Interest

This list is not exhaustive – there will be clubs/societies local to the reader.

The Gauge O Guild

The Gauge One Model Railway Association

Association of 16mm Narrow Gauge Modellers

The Gauge 3 Society

The G Scale Society

Appendix 10

Websites of Interest – includes suppliers, societies & manufacturers.

This list is not exhaustive and readers will likely find additional sites suited to their specific needs.

The Garden Railway Club - www.gardenrailwayclub.com

Garden Railway Specialists - www.grsuk.com

Association of 16mm Narrow Gauge Modellers - www.16mm.org.uk

The G Scale Society – www.gscalesociety.com

Scottish Garden Railways - http://www.gardentrains.co.uk

Dream Steam - www.dreamsteam.co.uk

Brandbright: Garden Railways - www.brandbright.co.uk

Kent Garden Railways - www.gardenrailways.com

Charles Ro Supply - ww.charlesro.com

TrainWorld - www.trainworld.com

Marklin Online Shop - www.maerklinshop.de

Massoth Decoders - www.massoth.com/index.en.html

Phoenix Decoders - www.phoenixsound.com/support/download.html

Zimo Decoders - www.zimo.at/web2010/sound/tableindex_EN.htm

LGB service Manuals - www.modeltrainforum.com/showthread.php?t=2974

USA Trains - www.usatrains.com/

Slaters – www.slatersplastikard.com

Aristo-Craft Service Drawings - www.aristocraftforum.com/viewtopic.php?f=23&t=21338

Bachmann Trains Parts Drawings - www.bachmanntrains.com/home-usa/references.php

Piko - www.piko.de/DE/index.php/de

RailBoss - www.gscalegraphics.net

Appendix 11

Scales & Conversion

I have recently found a very useful piece of software for converting almost everything to almost everything concerning model railways, including garden railways. Full details can be found at:

https://stanstrains.com/SoftwareHandyConverter.htm

Conversions include:

Any Scale to Another Scale
Scale Rulers
Drills & Screws size & conversion
Gradients
Scale Speed
Wiring size against power requirements
Metric Units to US Units & Reverse
LED Calculator
DCC C V's
Scale Figures
Scale Lumber
Scale Shapes & Strips
Shopping List
1:1 to Model RR Scale & Reverse
Ohm's Law
Resistor Calculator
Temperature & Weight
Thermal Rail Expansion
Large Scale Track
Minimum Track Radius
Helix Calculator
History
Curvature
Notes
Calculator
Plus, plus

While it is of US origin it is a very useful bit of software and can be downloaded from the site shown above – however it is not free currently (2018) costing $19.95 – the software requires Windows 7 and higher to Windows 10 and will also work with Mac.

While on the subject of scale it may be worth noting the size of a scale mile for the various garden railway scales.

	0 Gauge	Gauge 1	G scale
	1:48	1:36	1:32
1 scale mile equals	110ft	146ft 8 in	165ft